FOOD AND FARMING IN
PREHISTORIC
BRITAIN

FOOD AND FARMING IN
PREHISTORIC
BRITAIN

PAUL ELLIOTT

FONTHILL

Fonthill Media Language Policy

Fonthill Media publishes in the international English language market. One language edition is published worldwide. As there are minor differences in spelling and presentation, especially with regard to American English and British English, a policy is necessary to define which form of English to use. The Fonthill Policy is to use the form of English native to the author. Paul Elliott was born and educated in the UK and now lives in Yorkshire; therefore British English has been adopted in this publication.

Fonthill Media Limited
Fonthill Media LLC
www.fonthillmedia.com
office@fonthillmedia.com

First published in the United Kingdom and the United States of America 2016

British Library Cataloguing in Publication Data:
A catalogue record for this book is available from the British Library

Typeset in 10pt on 13pt Sabon
Printed and bound by CPI Group (UK) Ltd, Croydon, CR0 4YY

CONTENTS

INTRODUCTION

Food is a great link to the past. While written records, surviving artefacts, and the remains of buildings give us a sense of what life must have been like for people at a particular point in history, tasting a dish from that time provides us with unrivalled immediacy. Tastes and smells bring part of daily routine vividly to life in a way that the empty halls of a medieval castle or roofless Roman barrack block cannot.

For anyone interested in British prehistory, some of the buildings and artefacts that do remain can be enigmatic and difficult to interpret. Maiden Castle, the huge hill fort of the Iron Age Durotriges tribe, is 19 hectares of sinuous bank and ditch defence with no Iron Age building remains visible at all. What was once a thriving social and political centre and home to hundreds of people, is now a bare, grassy hill, home only to a herd of sheep. Neither the flat central area, where the houses and huts of the inhabitants once stood, nor the visually striking and steeply cut chalk ramparts remotely resemble their appearance during the hill fort's heyday. Lesser sites may not even be recognizable as manmade objects, and a great many prehistoric remains survive as nothing more than seasonal crop marks, stains in the soil, or readings on geophysical surveys.

What does remain, however, is the detritus of life: broken pottery, post holes, quern stones used for grinding the daily bread, fire-blackened stones that once surrounded a hearth, and tools—either of flint or iron, depending on the period. Life around the family hearth, daily life that probably continued unaltered for millennia, can be studied and recreated; all the evidence is there. In a way this enduring institution, the prehistoric household, transcended the changes in religious practice, barrow building, tribal politics, or metallurgy. The same local sources of food were gathered, stored, prepared, and cooked throughout the centuries. *Food and Farming in Prehistoric Britain* will explore the range of foods that were available to the prehistoric family and suggest a number of prehistoric recipes. Without a Roman gourmet writer like Apicius to guide us, we must instead look at traditional methods of preparing these foods. How were they cooked? What tools were used? How were they

:d, and most importantly of all, what did they taste like? This is not a prehistoric cookbook, though. The story of how families survived is a fascinating one, from the techniques used to hunt deer and wild boar during the Mesolithic, to the way in which crops were grown, processed, and stored. The roundhouse was fundamentally a farmhouse, both a dwelling and a work space, with a division of labour between men and women and between adults and children.

Chapter 1 provides a brief account of British prehistory from the end of the last ice age, when humans recolonized the landscape, through to the henge builders of the Neolithic and the barrow builders of the Bronze Age. The narrative ends with the climax of the British Iron Age and the defeat of the tribes by Roman invaders. British prehistory has for some time been divided up into several major periods, with approximate dates attributed to them. Those of interest to us, and provided here for reference, are:

Mesolithic Age	9000 BC to 4200 BC
Neolithic Age	4200 to *c.* 2200 BC
Early Bronze Age	2500 BC to 1500 BC
Middle Bronze Age	1500 BC to 1000 BC
Late Bronze Age	1000 BC to 700 BC
Iron Age	700 BC to the Roman invasion of AD 43

These are extremely broad divisions, used throughout the book to provide a reference point for readers; however, some of the great changes in prehistoric land use and construction overlap these rather neat categories.

The term 'Celtic' is often used in popular literature to describe the Iron Age period across Britain and the rest of Western Europe, and it serves as a useful label. At one time it was associated with a distinct people who were thought to have invaded Britain *en masse* and elsewhere, displacing the local Bronze Age population. It was thought the Celtic invaders brought their language and culture with them at the start of the Iron Age.

The Celtic language was certainly adopted by the Britons, suggesting a large influx of Celtic speakers at some point. Pots and swords, distinctive of a particular people, might be traded from one tribe to another and then adopted by them, without any invasion at all. But language is different and nearly always points to immigration or invasion. Tacitus tells us that there was little difference in language between British tribes living on the south coast and tribes living in Gaul. However, archaeologists find no evidence for large scale immigration or invasion at the start of the Iron Age and instead look further back, to periods of upheaval or transformation in British prehistory. Celtic migration might have occurred at the start of the early Bronze Age when a radical new style of pottery, new burial rites, and, of course, a new metal were all introduced simultaneously. However, it is more likely that Celtic peoples arrived in Britain much later, around 1500 BC. This was a revolutionary period in British prehistory, and the society that developed from it lasted until the late Iron Age and the coming of Rome. Some academics have suggested that the 'grandfather language' of all European tongues, known as Proto Indo-European, might well have arrived in Britain centuries earlier to usher in the British Bronze Age.

As long as we remember that 'Celtic speaker' does not equate to 'Celtic migrant' we are on safe ground, just as when we talk about Roman towns or Roman food. The number of actual Romans in Gaul, Britain, Spain, and elsewhere was comparatively small. The local populations were still there and Roman ways, from fashion to food, culture to beliefs, were adopted by those living under Roman rule. In this context we use 'Roman' as a cultural label, rather than a racial one. So, although things in the British Isles were sometimes done a little differently (such as the construction of houses that were round, not rectangular), the culture was Celtic—in fashion, in religion, in language, in art, and material culture. As new styles of art spread through the Celtic world from its heartland in the foothills of the Alps, they crossed the Channel and were, in turn, adopted by the British tribes.

Food and Farming in Prehistoric Britain neatly divides into two halves with the first exploring the world of prehistoric farming and the second half focusing on recipes and cooking techniques used within prehistoric households. Of course, in an age without writing, there are no surviving cookbooks from this era. Instead I have brought together available ingredients from British prehistory in ways that make sense, and, in many cases, that have persisted as traditional recipes throughout northern Europe. You will not find the recipes in this book adapted to the modern-day kitchen, the methods used come directly from the roundhouse and fire-pit and are offered in that spirit. As a concession, metric values are provided, but while cooking most of these dishes I simply approximated the ingredients that I needed. This, I feel, is the roundhouse way.

A quick glance at the appendix will illustrate the crippling restrictions that a modern cook will find placed upon himself. Nearly all of the vegetables, herbs, and fruits that we take for granted in our kitchens today were later imports, brought to our shores either by the Roman trade network, the Anglo-Saxons, or by later Tudor explorers. Food that one associates with traditional British cookery—the cabbage, potato, leek, and sprout, for example, were unknown to our Neolithic and Bronze Age ancestors. Recipes included in this book have to be mindful of the available ingredients, they also have to respect the cooking techniques used in the prehistoric roundhouse—oven-baking is out. The roaring fire and glowing embers of the hearth are the tools upon which we must depend in order to cook the majority of our foods.

A good deal of the advice gathered together within these pages has been learned first-hand through experimentation and experience. This journey of exploration would have been a lonely one had it not been for the good friends who have accompanied me. Meeting many years ago as Roman re-enactors, we all yearned to 'get back to basics' and to enjoy the simple pleasures of family life around a roundhouse fire. Together, the research, hard work, and desire for an authentic hot meal drove us on.

I would like to thank Lee and Sarah Steele who provided valuable advice on pot cookery; a number of my cook pots were made by Lee. I also owe a debt of gratitude to Alex and Gary Shaw, John Brayshaw, Jamie Mclean, Christine Elliott, and John Elliott for their advice and assistance, and for their feedback. Without diners waiting to taste the finished dish, the cook is merely going through the motions. Has it worked? Does it taste good? What should we try next? How did you get it to taste like that? Working simultaneously on different cookery projects, we were able to explore a huge number of recipes and cooking techniques from the prehistoric past through to the end of the Roman occupation. Alex's recipe for lamb stew, Gary's version of bean fritters, and Jamie's delicious beef and beer stew, all appear in this book. Finally I must also mention Roman cookery expert Sally Grainger, with whom I discussed ancient cooking methods, the late Paul Atkin, who made my wooden bowls, and the staff and volunteers of Ryedale Folk Museum at Hutton-le-Hole in North Yorkshire.

Paul Elliott

1

BRITISH PREHISTORY

Who the first inhabitants of Britain were, whether natives or immigrants remains obscure; one must remember we are dealing with barbarians.

Tacitus, Agricola 2

A sensible place to begin the history, or prehistory, of Britain is the end of the last ice age, during which vast and hostile ice sheets blanketed the country. For tens of thousands of years these ice sheets prevented humans from settling here; it was only as the ice melted and retreated that plant and animal life began to slowly take hold. Into this chilly tundra landscape stepped the first Britons, whose flint tools suggest an origin in the Low Countries. The open tundra plains of 12,500 BC were still home to mammoth and giant deer.

By 9500 BC the climate had warmed sufficiently for birch, pine, and hazel trees to take root in Britain, effectively transforming the post-glacial steppe into a vast deciduous woodland. Into this forested landscape came red deer, wild horse and cattle, elk (known as moose to the Americans), wolf, bear, wild boar, and even lynx. Hot on their heels were groups of human hunter-gatherers who were drawn to these lands by the promise of abundant prey and edible plant life. These groups, these families, of intrepid hunters were entering an uninhabited wilderness and had to rely on their wits, their resilience, and the skills they brought with them to survive. The climate at the start of this period, known as the Mesolithic (or Middle Stone Age), was a little cooler than today, probably resembling that of Scotland or southern Scandinavia. Trees of oak, beech, and ash (the hardwoods) were latecomers to these Mesolithic woodlands.

Mesolithic (9000 BC to 4200 BC)

Do not imagine these first bands of hunters paddling across the Channel to Dover. A vast amount of seawater was still locked up in ice sheets further north, and as a result sea levels were much lower, enabling the Mesolithic groups to walk across to Britain. Low-lying marshlands and reed swamps spread out across what is now the North Sea forming 'Doggerland', a fertile plain filled with hunting opportunities. Although the nets of trawlers often pull up artefacts from this lost world below the waves, archaeologists are unsure how many people lived there. In all likelihood Doggerland formed the focus of life for the hunting communities of the north and as sea levels rose throughout the Mesolithic, the rocky uplands of the lands we know as Britain provided a retreat from the threatening waves.

Sites in Britain known to have been used by Mesolithic bands seem to have been occupied only at certain times of the year. The hunters moved on to other locations where prey or wild plants were known to thrive at certain times of the year. In this way the groups were always moving on to new resources—resources that were annually replenished. For much of the time these hunter-gatherers seem to have lived in portable or temporary shelters, much like the Yukaghir of Siberia. However, the recent discovery of permanent houses at Howick in Northumbria, Queensferry in Scotland, and at Star Carr in North Yorkshire indicate that some sites were probably occupied throughout the year, and for decades.

Star Carr is crucial for our understanding of life in the Mesolithic. Only twenty minutes' drive from my own house, this ancient hunting settlement was once sited on the edge of a large glacial lake, called Lake Flixton. Nothing remains of the lake today—it had silted up by the end of the Mesolithic. The dense birch woodland and reed banks that once surrounded it, as well as the wild fowl and deer that roamed its shoreline, have also gone, to be replaced by modern field systems and drainage ditches. Here, *circa* 9000 BC, a large timber platform had been constructed at the water's edge and used as the centre for hunting and fishing activities. Tools of flint, antler, and bone were found at the site, along with animal bones, a paddle (suggestive of a boat), and barbed spear and arrow points. Remarkably, a house has recently been excavated on drier ground, away from the shore, and Nicky Milner, site director at Star Carr, suspects that there are probably several more houses at the site.

Life in Mesolithic Britain was small scale, groups of related families travelling together from one site to another as the seasons dictated, hunting game and gathering edible plants, berries, and nuts. They would split up and then meet one another later on in the year. Everyone would have been a hunter or a gatherer (or both), everyone would be able to work wood and flint, and to twist plant fibres to manufacture twine and make basketry. These were essential skills of survival. Clothing consisted of animal skins that were carefully tailored to fit and sewn up with animal gut. To bring down their prey, the Mesolithic hunters used bows, harpoons, and spears, and reached the perfect ambush position either by foot, or dug-out canoe.

Was life in the Stone Age 'poor, nasty, brutish and short' (to quote the seventeenth-century philosopher Thomas Hobbes)? These hunter-gatherers, like many nomadic tribes today, still had time to create art, to carve elaborate designs into paddles or pieces of antler, and to engage in religious practices that helped bind their communities together. There is evidence for the belief in ancestor spirits, and even for spirit-priests or shamans.

Did this religion extend to the construction of temples? The substantial houses already mentioned may themselves have served as holy places, just as more recent hunting communities in Patagonia live in temporary structures, but build more substantial buildings for their religious ceremonies. But they might just as easily have been used for long-term habitation. On my last visit to Stonehenge, Britain's famous Neolithic monument, I must have baffled a group of tourists in the car park who were disembarking from their tour coach. While the enigmatic stones stood right behind me, just across the busy A344, I was instead kneeling down to take photographs of markings painted on the tarmac by the local council. Three circles of white paint denote the precise location of three post holes dated to the Mesolithic, thousands of years before work on the much later Stonehenge monument had begun. These holes were sunk for three huge pine posts, all between 60 and 80 cm in diameter. It is generally agreed that these posts were probably carved, much like North American totem poles, and that the straight-line alignment of the posts had a religious meaning. Yet the posts date back to around 8000 BC, they show us that the Mesolithic was far more than some desperate struggle for existence. One, or most likely more than one, community of early Britons, came together for several days or weeks to construct this imposing timber alignment. It is certainly no coincidence that Stonehenge sits only metres away from the site of this ancient timber alignment. Mesolithic hunter-gatherers marked out that point in the landscape as a holy site, a site that continued to retain an aura of mystery and magic, for 6,000 years more.

Neolithic (4200 BC to 2200 BC)

By 6000 BC, the rising waters of the North Sea had flooded the rich hunting grounds of Doggerland and cut the British Isles off from continental Europe. However, this inundation did not cut Britain off from new ideas and innovations. In the centuries after 4500 BC, immigrants crossed from France and brought with them animals, seed corn, and the knowledge of farming. This was not an invasion, but seems to have involved small groups of farmers moving in to clear and then cultivate the land. Once here, their ideas spread and indigenous British hunter-gatherers began to switch from their nomadic existence to one of cattle herding and cultivation. Communities settled down into permanent or semi-permanent farm houses, and they adopted a new style of flint working that included broad blades and polished stone axes. Where these new tools are found, they are usually associated with the bones of domesticated animals and shards of pottery—another new innovation from the Continent.

Early farmers may have continued to hunt and gather in the traditional manner for some parts of the year, but eventually the indigenous Britons were all lured by the farming lifestyle. Some aspects of agriculture had already been adopted by the hunter-gatherers: they had domesticated dogs, they were using fire to clear vegetation, they processed certain plant seeds to make flour, and they coppiced hazel and willow trees in order to secure a source of long, straight poles.

Why did these independent and mobile groups swap hunting and gathering for farming? Farming requires that a community stay in one place for much of the year, it requires hard work to clear forest, break the soil, sow seed, manage animals, and harvest crops. It also requires manpower—the more hands on the farm, the more land could be cultivated and so a population explosion naturally coincided with the start of the Neolithic. Was life as a hunter so bad? Was the availability of game on the decline? Increasing competition for resources must have forced families to look at new ways of securing sources of food. We should not ignore the fact, too, that farming was a social development that further extended a community's control over its environment. We should not perceive the Mesolithic hunter as a 'noble savage', perfectly at peace with, and attuned to, the natural world. As we have seen, these communities worked hard to manipulate the world around them; farming provided even more control, and gave these clans and tribes more power over their own destiny.

It is interesting to note that some of these Neolithic settlements were established on previously occupied Mesolithic camps. These are the same communities, changing their ways, adapting to a new shift in society. Soon after 4000 BC these settled communities begin investing vast amounts of manpower in the building of impressive monuments. What they built provides a host of clues about the new way of life. These 'causewayed enclosures' began to spread across southern Britain, and they match similar monuments found throughout northern Europe. Each causewayed enclosure is an area of flat ground, usually on the brow of a hill and surrounded by a series of concentric ditches. At many places around their circuits, these ditches are crossed by earthen causeways, allowing access to the centre from many different directions. Serving primarily as meeting places for neighbouring communities, these enclosures could serve a variety of other purposes. Examples such as Hambledon Hill, Dorset, and Windmill Hill, Wiltshire, were used to deposit offerings within ritual burials. It is likely that separate families held claim to different stretches of the ditch and returned at different times throughout the year to make new offerings to the gods.

The design of the enclosures, and the apparent lack of substantial Neolithic houses or villages, suggests that the new farmers were mainly cattle herders. Causewayed enclosures allowed clans to bring their herds together in order to breed, to trade with one another, to make alliances, to feast, arrange weddings, to bury the dead, and welcome new adults into the community. In a vast landscape, these scattered cattle farmers could re-establish links, just as they had in the old days, when they had broken the hunt to meet up with groups of relatives.

In the early third millennium, causewayed enclosures were abandoned in favour of 'henges', which were circular ditch and bank monuments, typically situated on lowland sites. These circular meeting places still served as social gathering points and places where rituals and ceremonies that were important to the community could be enacted. The heads of families and clans in the neighbourhood would be able to meet at the henges and tombs, perhaps to discuss differences or make plans for the future.

Neolithic tombs were communal and are typified by the chambered long barrow, a cluster of stone chambers that was covered by a long earthen barrow mound. Access was made through an entrance with its own ritual courtyard, and it seems that meetings and ceremonies held there would involve the removal of certain bones of the ancestors. These bones were the levers of power, bringing the weight of the ancestors to bear on very real, earthly problems. Once the ceremony was completed the bones, like the bones of Christian saints locked away in their golden reliquaries, seem to have been returned to their place in the stone chamber.

As the Neolithic progressed, the population expanded, and so did the need for farmland and for sources of decent flint. Forest was felled with polished axes to make room for cattle pasture and cropland, and increasing numbers of long barrows, burial cairns, and henges were constructed. Territories were being marked out and communities were 'joining up' with a series of trackways and communal henges. Some of these henges, like Avebury in Wiltshire, Arbor Low in Derbyshire, and the Ring of Brodgar in Orkney, featured a new phenomenon—the stone circle. Meanwhile, borders and frontiers were also being recognised, and it was to be the barrows and burial cairns that helped to mark out the edges of these new tribal areas.

Flint was now needed on a prodigious scale, and full-scale mining began at locations like Cissbury hill fort and Harrow Hill, both in Sussex, and of course at the extensive mine workings of Grimes Graves, Norfolk. Flint was extracted and then transported or traded long distances across Britain's growing network of trackways. Good stone suitable for making sharp, polished axes was also in great demand and the few places able to produce it were found in Cornwall, Wales, the Lake District, and Northern Ireland. These remote outcrops on Britain's western shores were identified and exploited,

Flint tools. The three tools on the right are scrapers from Oldbury Camp, Wiltshire. The nine flints on the left are from Flamborough Head, East Yorkshire. Row one is composed of scrapers, useful in cleaning animal hides or working wood, row two contains piercers and hole borers, which, as the name suggests, were used to bore holes into wood, leather, bone, or antler. The long tool is a 'fabricator', perhaps the head of a pick or digging tool, and beneath this are a Bronze Age tanged arrowhead and a leaf-shaped Neolithic arrowhead. (*Author's collection*)

and they were no doubt chosen for their spectacular location as much as for the quality of their stone. Axes from these areas were traded the length and breadth of Britain. The quern stone, that essential tool of every prehistoric household, was also quarried from suitable outcrops and similarly traded. In the Neolithic and the Bronze Age, these grindstones were saddle-shaped, and required a top stone to be rocked back and forth over the lower stone, crushing the grain between them and producing flour.

Houses from the Neolithic are hard to find, but those so far discovered are generally rectangular in shape, with a central hearth and a single doorway. Recent discoveries at Durrington Walls, close to Stonehenge, have uncovered hundreds of houses that were all built to a similar ground plan. The Durrington houses resembled those found in 1850 at Skara Brae, Orkney, although the latter were impressive stone-built affairs, while those at Durrington were post-built, probably with thatched roofs. Evidence for furniture was found in both, in particular box-beds flanking the doorway and the inclusion of a 'dresser' or family shrine on the back wall. The similarity in layout between dwellings

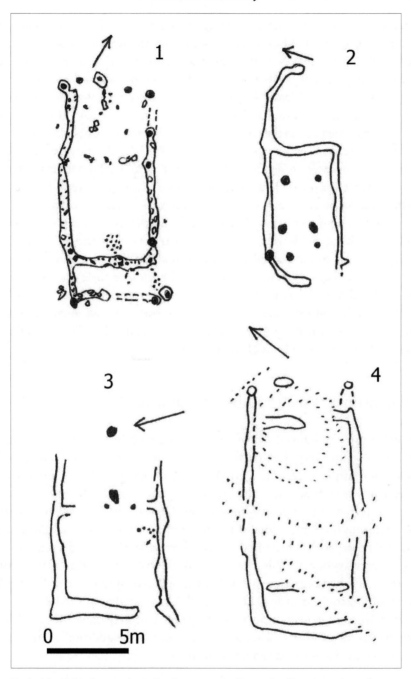

Early Neolithic houses in Ireland; arrows indicate the direction of north.
1. Ballyglass, County Mayo.
2. Ballygalley, County Antrim.
3. Newtown, County Cork.
4. Tankardstown, County Meath.
(*C. Malone*)

as far apart as Scotland and Wiltshire, the construction of henges to a similar pattern throughout the British Isles, along with the identification of pottery 'fashions' suggests that Neolithic communities were not insular and poverty stricken, eking out a miserable existence of agricultural toil and back-breaking labour. Instead, the evidence suggests a series of interconnected farming clans, dependant on cattle rearing and wheat cultivation. Beliefs and fashions were shared and carried across the land via tracks and rivers and coastal voyages.

Enough agricultural surplus existed to free up the large amount of collective manpower needed to build the great communal monuments. There is no evidence for great chiefs, tyrants, or lords, however; Neolithic society seems to have been governed by the families themselves, probably led by family elders who met at regular periods and at large seasonal gatherings. Violence, raiding, and warfare certainly occurred. There is evidence of a battle or siege of some sort at Hambledon Hill around 2850 BC and also at Crickley Hill, Gloucestershire, where the causewayed enclosure there was repeatedly attacked and rebuilt, to be finally abandoned in the middle of the Neolithic. As the population expanded, friction and tensions between communities naturally developed, alongside good relations and alliances. No one could go back to the relative freedoms of the Mesolithic.

Early Bronze Age (2500 BC to 1500 BC)

Of all the greatest innovations of mankind, agriculture and the use of metals must rank at the very top. Yet the first introductions of metal into British society initially caused only a ripple. The first metal to be liberated from the earth was copper, and a distinct Copper Age can be detected in some Near Eastern and European communities. Ötzi, the prehistoric man found mummified in the Alps, belonged to this Copper age. His body, clothing, and personal possessions, when lifted out of the ice in 1991, showed a remarkable level of preservation, teaching us a great deal. Ötzi the 'Ice Man' dated from 3300 BC and had been carrying a small copper axe at the time of his death, along with a tool kit of flint blades. Following rapidly on the heels of the Copper Age, and in many places leap-frogging it entirely, came bronze. While copper had its uses it was a rather soft metal, but the addition of tin to the crucible created a much harder alloy—bronze.

Early Bronzework

Bronze was an expensive product, available only to the elites (like the leaders of clans sitting on the most important trade routes). Small amounts of copper, bronze, and increasing amounts of gold find their way into individual burials. Along with bronze technology came a new type of pottery, the Beaker, and with it an association of new, fashionable items such as tanged arrowheads of flint, the wrist guards worn by bowmen, metal daggers, and jewellery.

One theory suggests that a Beaker 'package' or Beaker culture spread across the Channel from Europe, but the changes that occurred through the Early Bronze Age are so striking that an influx of newcomers seems very likely. The Amesbury Archer, a Bronze Age man buried close to Stonehenge around 2300 BC, probably grew up in the Alps according to oxygen isotope analysis on his tooth enamel.

The earliest Beaker burials were located some distance from the large henge monuments of Britain. It seems that Beaker folk were initially outside the mainstream of established Neolithic society. According to Mike Parker Pearson, 'their lifestyle, their politics, their social structure, [were] so very different to the host culture within Britain'. Beaker immigrants came from parts of Europe that did not have great communal projects and collective power structures, they were not prepared to work *en masse* for the good of the community. Things were changing. With their new metals and new social order, the Beaker people brought with them a dispersed, decentralised social structure. The whole rationale for the henges and other communal monuments quickly disappeared.

For reasons still unknown, Britons soon abandoned their rectangular, Neolithic houses and instead began building round houses. This form of domestic dwelling continued in use through to the Roman invasion, 2,000 years later. Still, the remains of houses are relatively rare during this period, leading many archaeologists to suggest that the Neolithic emphasis on cattle rearing, supplemented by wheat and barley production, continued

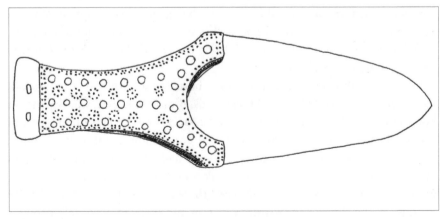

Early Bronze Age dagger complete with its wooden hilt that has been decorated with bronze pins and rivets. From a burial at Milston, Wiltshire. (*J. F. S. Stone*)

into the Early Bronze Age. The grand burial of a Beaker man, excavated at Irthlingborough, Northamptonshire, seems to add weight to this theory. He was buried in true Beaker fashion, with a pottery Beaker (of course), a flint arrowhead and flint dagger, a stone wrist guard, a boar's tusk, an amber ring, a couple of pebbles (one of them chalk), and a few flint tools. Most remarkable, though, was the mountain of cattle bones above the body which included 184 skulls, fifteen pelvises, thirty-three shoulder blades, and thirty-eight jawbones. When analysed, the bones told researchers that the cattle had been young bullocks, at their prime for meat yield. Most likely, these bones represent the remains of a great funerary feast and the cattle brought to the burial site from the herd of the dead man's family, or assembled by mourners each bringing their own offering. However it is interpreted, it is clear that huge numbers of cattle were available in the Nene Valley at that period.

Beakers are wonderful things, certainly of a size to be used (and probably owned) by one person alone. They are of a sinuous form, with an S-shaped profile and many are eggshell thin. All are intricately decorated with impressed geometric designs made by bird bones, cord, or sharp twigs. Perhaps the most fascinating aspect of the Beakers and Beaker culture, is the fact that pollen grains from lime flowers were found in a beaker excavated in a grave near Fife, Scotland. The beaker had probably been filled with mead—a drink of fermented honey—that was placed with the body of the deceased as an offering. Did alcohol arrive with the Beaker people? Or did it signify a new social trend that had alcohol at its heart? Whatever it meant, the Beaker was the drinking cup of an individual, whereas the pottery and bowls of the Neolithic were for communal consumption only.

Gradually, the evidence for the cult of individuality that arrived with the Beaker intensified. The Early Bronze Age is famous for the erection of the immense sarsen trilithons at Stonehenge. Although this marks the last hurrah for that important and incredibly ancient henge, it signals a whole new era of monumental construction. Stone circles, standing stones, stone alignments, and elaborate grave mounds were all being erected by the new elite of bronze owning, Beaker-using, leaders.

In the Neolithic, land had formed the basis for wealth and communities could generally provide for all of their needs. Bronze, however, was dependant both on highly skilled specialists as well as access to supplies of copper and tin. Trade and travel, therefore, assumed greater and greater importance. Families who controlled trade routes, or who had alliances with tribes rich in bronze, were able to flaunt their wealth. Personal items fashioned from bronze or gold became status symbols amongst these families. The Beaker folk had introduced the concept of wealth to Britain and this had inevitably brought with it inequalities and social divisions; the Irthlingborough burial perfectly illustrates this new social order. Buried in the ground, just before the barrow was erected, was the body of a young man, and his only grave good was a single bone needle, quite a contrast to that of the man buried above him in the round barrow. Was he a servant? Was he a son or another family member? The grave goods of the primary burial indicated the growing complexity that the Beaker culture had brought with it. The finger-sized chalk pebble had come all the way from the Stonehenge area, while the flint dagger had been manufactured in Norfolk. The amber had been imported from the Baltic Sea and the jet buttons from Whitby, on the Yorkshire coast.

Beaker burials occur singly within round barrows or cairns and number some 30,000 in Britain alone. These barrows have no chamber, there was no access to the bones within once the dead were buried; the concept of a large communal tomb was abandoned. Wealthy individuals were now buried alone. Yet communities are still represented within these monuments. Often 'secondary burials' occur, where the remains of a cremated body is placed within an urn and then buried within the upper levels of an existing round barrow. In addition, many Beaker barrows are usually found in groups of between four and forty, so-called 'barrow cemeteries'. What does this mean? Round barrows probably represent a single family, and serve almost the same purpose as a family chapel within a church, or as a private mausoleum. The rest of the population were either put into unmarked cremation cemeteries or into an existing round barrow as a secondary cremation burial. Where once the tribe had worked collectively, now power and influence was held by the heads of wealthy families.

Bush Barrow, excavated in 1808, illustrates well the type of burials occurring at this time. Located only 1 km from the freshly erected sarsen stones of Stonehenge, the occupant of Bush Barrow was a man who had been laid to rest with three bronze daggers, one of which had a hilt studded with hundreds of gold nails. Accompanying the daggers was a bronze axe, a stone mace, a golden belt buckle, and a remarkable lozenge-shaped golden sheet. Bush Barrow man was obviously someone of status and influence. The number of metal daggers in his possession and the presence of so much gold illustrate his wealth, while the mace (complete with decorative bone inlays for the handle) is a testament to his rank or influence.

Perhaps the most remarkable aspect of the Early Bronze Age is that, amidst all of the turbulence and change, the great monuments of the Neolithic continued to be used. Not only that, but many were extended and dramatically upgraded with stone circles. The final phases of Stonehenge and Avebury in Wiltshire, are the most spectacular examples of this process, and they form the heart of a rich religious complex. Marking a crucial change from a Neolithic community of equals to one dominated by elite families and competition, the Early Bronze Age is incredibly important. It ushered in not just new materials and technologies, but a new society. It also set a trend in prehistoric Britain that would be played out over the course of the next 2,000 years.

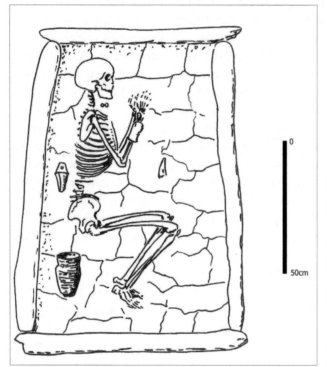

Early Bronze Age grave at Kellythorpe, near Driffield, East Yorkshire. The grave contained some of the key pieces of the 'Beaker package' including an archer's wrist guard, Bell Beaker drinking vessel, copper dagger, and amber buttons. (*J. R. Mortimer*)

Middle Bronze Age (1500 BC to 1000 BC)

Subdividing the Bronze Age might seem to be splitting hairs, but the fact is that the system of 'metal ages' is not a neat and tidy one, it was originally devised by the early antiquarians who required a method for sorting and categorizing their growing collections of ancient artefacts. It was Christian Jurgensen Thomsen, a Dane, who established in 1836 that the age of iron had been preceded by an age of bronze, which had in turn been preceded by an age of stone. Difficulties arose when later archaeologists began to see social developments that overlapped or occurred within the three-age system. It has been clear for some time that a major farming revolution occurred in the middle of the Bronze Age, a century or so either side of 1500 BC.

Bronze is seen in predominance during the Middle Bronze Age, flint axes are replaced at all levels by a myriad of bronze types, and tools other than axes also begin to be manufactured from this now long-established alloy. Cross-Channel vessels like the extraordinary Dover Boat, dating from 1500 BC, facilitated this accelerating trade in axes. The evidence suggests that bronze was now in common circulation and no longer in the hands of certain powerful families.

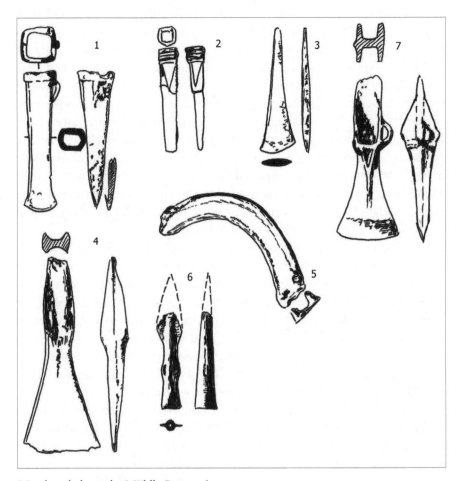

Metalwork from the Middle Bronze Age.
1. Socketed axe (from the Taunton hoard).
2. Socketed punch (also from the Taunton hoard).
3. Chisel from Sparkford, Somerset.
4. Flanged palstave, Barton Bendish, Norfolk.
5. Knobbed sickle from Edington Burtle, Somerset.
6. Side-looped spearhead, Stump Bottom, Sussex.
7. Palstave from Edington Burtle.
C. *Burgess*)

Yet the transformation that occurred was not material, but social, religious, and economic. Throughout the Early Bronze Age the population had been increasing and communities had been evolving rapidly to cope. By 1500 BC this population pressure had reached crisis point, and the farming economy that had been established by those first Neolithic immigrants needed a complete overhaul. Perhaps the most dramatic change was the total abandonment of the great henges, the long cursus monuments and even the ubiquitous round Beaker barrows. The mechanics of belief took a dramatic turn, away from grand solar alignments and vast ritual landscapes, to small-scale water cults. A warmer climate encouraged the cultivation of previously inhospitable uplands; Dartmoor, the Pennines and the Peak District, the North Yorkshire Moors, and western and central Scotland were all colonized by Bronze Age farmers. When the climate then deteriorated around 1200 BC, these upland pioneers were forced back down to the lowlands.

Farming was not just spreading outwards and upwards, but there was also a degree of intensification. The Middle Bronze Age provides evidence in abundance for the widespread laying out of field systems, not just for the grazing of sheep and cattle, but also for the growing of crops. While arable farmland has been identified within the Neolithic period, it appears piecemeal and difficult to identify. Now field systems become extensive, the land parcelled up and subdivided with boundaries that have persisted (in some places) through to the modern day. Communal labour on the large ritual henges was instead redirected toward these new field systems.

Society changed too. The earlier Beaker barrows had sat in rows, often on ridges, with their high-status occupants looking out over the landscape that they had dominated in life. After 1500 BC, small cemetery clusters replace barrow building, these are local affairs with very little outward presence. Communities were being reorganised around the new field systems with the result that farms and roundhouses from this period proliferate in the archaeological record. Gatherings also become local affairs. Perhaps with the move away from cattle rearing and pastoralism the Britons no longer needed big community gathering places such as henges. Communication with one's neighbours (and, one would imagine, one's cousins and more distant relatives) was now a matter of routine. Ritual gatherings were now conducted at the family level, rather than the tribal. Trade may have also been conducted at a local level, goods being exchanged with neighbouring communities or received as part of a marriage arrangement or other social obligation.

Flag Fen, near Peterborough, has proven to be a treasure trove of Bronze Age artefacts. Sat on the edge of ancient fenland, the Flag Fen site enjoyed great religious prestige. A timber trackway extended for 1 km from dry land over an inland sea, where it ended at a timber platform. From there objects of value were cast into the black waters below. Hundreds of bronze artefacts have been recovered from the mud around both the trackway and the platform including spears, tools, swords, daggers, axe heads, and even a pair of shears. Nearly all of these objects had been bent or broken, making them useless in this world, but not in the next. In 1937, workmen from the Trent Navigation Company were dredging the river at Clifton and came across a similar timber platform and a scatter of bronze items, including swords and daggers, all dated to around 1100 BC.

Prehistoric communities had always made offerings to the gods or the spirits, but in the Neolithic these had often been quern stones, ritual meals, pottery, human or animal bones, or simple pieces of jewellery. The very bones of the ancestors themselves served as objects of veneration. Now, with bronze and gold now on the scene, worshippers could offer the gods something spectacular. Most Bronze Age offerings were deposited into pools or rivers, rather than be buried in the ground as they had been in the Neolithic, and artefacts recovered from places like Flag Fen and Clifton were deliberately damaged to put them beyond the reach of man. Three of the Flag Fen swords, for example, were purposely and repeatedly smashed against a rock to blunt them, tips were broken off and the hilts removed. Some of these items show wear, and were almost certainly owned and used by the worshipper, while others seem to have been made especially for the ritual. This act of 'breaking' an object before giving it to the gods persisted into the Iron Age and is no different from the practice common throughout the ancient world of sacrificing an animal in honour of the gods. The spirit of the slaughtered beast, and the spirit of the broken sword (if you will) had to be sent on its way before the ancestor spirits or the gods could receive it.

But where did these gods or spirits actually dwell? In the Neolithic period, knowledge of solar alignments existed, particularly those that occurred at the summer and winter solstices. Yet the burial offerings of the period seem to suggest that the land of the dead existed below the ground, perhaps even within the earth itself. It has even been suggested (quite plausibly) that the excavation of the great ditches and embankments of the causewayed enclosures, henges, cursus, and barrow mounds were an integral (if not the central) part of the worship. A community came together to dig. If the tribal spirits or gods dwelt below the ground, then this activity made perfect sense.

Something radically changed in the century either side of 1500 BC. Britons quickly switched from burying objects in the ground to dropping them into sacred pools and rivers. Did this mark a change in religious thinking? Had the entire cosmology of Bronze Age Britain changed? Or had the new bronze offerings required some new method of disposal? Perhaps burial just was not the most effective way of sending an object to the gods. Reflective pools and still water could be seen as portals or windows into the underworld. Or (the cynic in me says) burying a bronze sword, worth a dozen head of cattle, was not thought to be safe. Dropping these objects into a pitch black pool or a swift-flowing river, however, certainly put the object beyond the realm of the living, making it extremely difficult for anyone else to recover it. It reached the gods, and was out of the easy reach of men. Prehistoric life was no idyll; poverty, hunger, and desperation would strike the population from time to time, just as they did during the Middle Ages. We have an image of uneducated peasants in ancient history kowtowing to the religious laws of their leaders. Yet the evidence from dynastic Egypt illustrates the lengths to which ordinary folk were willing to go to plunder the vast fortunes hidden away within the tombs of the Valley of the Kings.

During the Middle Bronze Age, some communities established themselves within hill forts. These fortified hilltop enclosures (like Harrow Hill and Norton Fitzwarren) were not the same as the causewayed enclosures of the early Neolithic. Ram's Hill, Berkshire, for example, dates from 1300 BC and features a heavily defended gateway that allowed entrance into an interior filled with roundhouses. Mike Parker Pearson believes that these early hill forts dominated the farmsteads and villages around them and probably acted as a local market for pottery, bronze work, and agricultural surplus. As the Bronze Age progressed these hill forts began to proliferate.

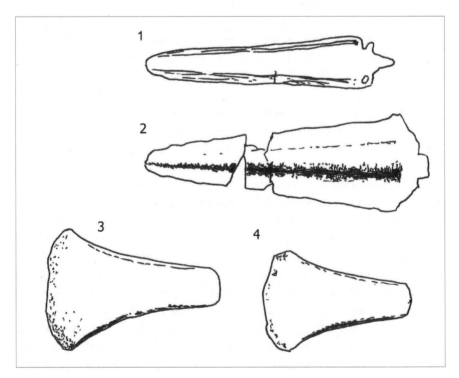

Metalwork from the Early Bronze Age, part of the Killaha East hoard, found in County Derry. (*C. Burgess*)

Late Bronze Age (1000 BC to 700 BC)

After 1000 BC the dead were first cremated and then buried in shallow pits without even a pot to hold the ashes. This was a new development. By 800 BC even these cremation burials vanish from the archaeological record, leaving us with no clue as to how or where the dead were disposed of.

Across the land, hilltop settlements were being constructed that must have served a defensive function. Gateways and ramparts are much in evidence, but it is suspected that they also played a role in social activity. Sheep and cattle may have been gathered there for fairs, marriages arranged, goods traded, religious rites observed, and meetings held between clans. We do not know whether these hill forts were built and controlled by the communities around them, or were owned and inhabited by a wealthy chief.

The pinnacle of Bronze Age development is characterised with the construction of defensive hill forts, and with the production of increasingly sophisticated weapons. Warfare had arrived in Britain and along with it a Bronze Age arms race. Daggers had been the fashion during the Early Bronze Age and eventually superseded as a status symbol by rapiers, long thin bronze swords, suitable only for stabbing. By the Late Bronze Age heavier bronze swords with leaf-shaped blades, typified by the Ewart Park type, were introduced and these could be used to hack and chop at an opponent as well as stab. Other styles of bronze swords, like the Carp's Tongue design, belonged to a European tradition. Spearheads follow their own train of development.

In the rest of Europe, warriors of the Late Bronze Age Urnfield culture produced bronze helmets, leg defences, and even breastplates for their warriors to wear into battle. Communication links across the length of Europe had never been better and Urnfield military equipment is very reminiscent of the type of arms and armour being used in Mycenaean Greece at this time. It has been suggested the Homeric duels between Greek warriors were a common feature of Late Bronze Age warfare across Europe. Bronze weaponry served as a symbol of social status, but was certainly used to wage war between communities, clans, and tribes. The skeletons of two men, found at Tormarton, Somerset, both displayed savage spear wounds, to the pelvis of one and through the spinal cord of the other.

Iron, a new metal that could be obtained from a number of different sources, was on the horizon. In fact, some iron tools were already being produced during Britain's Late Bronze Age, but metal production and the trade in raw materials was still focussed on copper and tin. When the widespread adoption of iron did occur, *c*. 700 BC, the fabric of British society and the pattern of settlement seems to have continued unabated. Indeed, taking a broad view of events in prehistory, the Middle and Late Bronze Ages seem to have formed the beginnings of a society that continued into the Iron Age. The new metal did not revolutionize British society. The real revolution had been agricultural and it had occurred back in 1500 BC.

Iron Age (700 BC to AD 43)

The Britain of the Late Bronze Age continued to develop, even as new methods of metal production took hold. Iron was now ubiquitous and even replaced the flint tools that had continued in use throughout the Bronze Age.

By 500 BC, hill forts existed right across Britain—close to 3,300 have so far been identified, many of which were built on prominent hills. Their position harkens back to those rows of Beaker barrows that sat up on high ridges, intended to be visible for miles around, not just to their builders in the farmland below, but also to travellers and neighbouring communities. Hill forts had this same intended purpose, to impress, to intimidate, and to carry with them the pride of the tribe that had built them. Chiefs and kings certainly existed when the Roman invasion took place, but these powerful leaders seem to have arisen as the Iron Age matured. Hill forts were fortified settlements, yet most of the roundhouses built within the ramparts are of roughly the same size. Nothing like an Iron Age palace or 'great hall' has ever been found at one of these sites, suggesting that, if there were warlords and chieftains earlier in the period, then they must have had some kind of mandate from the tribe. Like the building of causewayed enclosures or henges, these great hill forts would have required vast amounts of labour, provided by the communities that would use them. It is doubtful that the people 'lived in their shadow' as an Egyptian peasant might have looked up at the pyramids of Giza from his remote and humble place in the world. All the evidence suggests that hill settlements were used by the communities around them. When finds from large sites, like Danebury, are compared with much humbler dwellings, it is quite striking how similar they are. Spinning, leatherwork, bread making, weaving, pottery, and metalworking all took place at the greatest of hill forts, just as they did in roundhouses and villages across Britain. Clues to the hill fort's other activities have also been detected at Danebury; a collection of stone weights as well as iron ingots (known as 'currency bars') suggests these settlements served an important economic role as trading centres.

Over time a number of hill forts were abandoned while other sites were extended, enlarged, and aggrandized with multiple rampart defences of ditch and bank. Although a few of the interior spaces remained quite bare of dwellings, most were populated with roundhouses and some, like Danebury and Maiden Castle, could easily be described as towns. Typically, a hill fort featured two gateways at opposite ends of the enclosure. The steep-sided bank was frequently faced with timber or sometimes drystone walling, both as a statement and as a reinforcement. Around these rapidly growing social centres, large tribal areas began to coalesce and are visible in some of the pottery types of the Iron Age, which begin to show regional variations. These tribal units are given definite form, and even name, by the Romans prior to their arrival in AD 43.

It is easy to focus on the growing numbers of hill forts and the development of the large tribal entities that faced Julius Caesar and Aulus Plautius, but earlier Bronze Age trends continued. Extensive field systems had been laid out after *c.* 1500 BC, but in the Iron Age there is evidence from parts of southern Britain that territories were brought under even tighter control. Around Hampshire and Wiltshire, for example, long boundary ditches were dug to encompass large tracts of farmland. One of these ditches, running past Quarley hill fort, can be traced for up to 11 km. A number of these new ditch divisions terminate at hill forts, one of which is the 2-km stretch that connects the valley of the River Test to the hill settlement at Danebury. Taken together with other evidence, it is clear that Britain's population had increased dramatically since the Early Bronze Age. Innovations in metalworking had led to gradual efficiencies in agriculture that enabled the landscape to support many more people. Field boundaries had become necessary as conflict between communities that now existed closer than ever before soon became

Early Iron Age pottery from All Cannings Cross, Wiltshire. (*A. Wilkins*)

a part of life. While the hill forts and swords of the Bronze Age suggest that communities were going on the defensive, the warlike and battle-ready culture that emerged at the end of the Iron Age illustrates just how intensive the population pressures were becoming in the centuries leading up to the Roman invasion.

I have used the term hill fort quite liberally here; many communities in the British Iron Age built monuments that were certainly not hill forts, but must have played much the same role. In the north-east, hill forts are rare and much smaller 'fortified homesteads' were the norm, while in the eastern counties, from the East Riding of Yorkshire south to the Thames valley and East Anglia, the local people settled instead in large villages. The rugged Scottish landscape gave rise to a completely different form of Iron Age settlement. The roundhouse concept was adapted and reimagined in stone. Brochs are the famous drystone towers that include galleries within the thickness of their walls. They show a sophisticated knowledge of architecture in stone and often feature attached enclosures that were also built of the same material. Other northern building types include hill forts as in the lowland zone, but also duns, which are drystone fortifications that represent a single homestead, and wheelhouses, which are round houses in stone with internal radial subdivisions (like the spokes of a wheel). Finally, some of the Iron Age clans and tribes constructed artificial islands known as crannogs to serve as platforms for offshore dwellings. Whatever the form that settlements took, the trend throughout the Iron Age was for the construction of the permanent and visually dominant homestead.

Between 200 BC and 100 BC, the process of enlarging and elaborating hill forts stopped. In the south of England a number of lowland settlements were established instead that seem to have served a definite commercial or trading purpose. These open settlements are called *oppida* after a term used by Julius Caesar for similar sites that he had seen in Gaul. *Oppida*, like those at Wheathampstead, Winchester, and Bigbury are typically surrounded by a series of defensive earthworks; at many of these sites, Iron Age coins were also minted, further emphasizing their commercial importance. The *oppida* represent the beginnings of an urban system that was fully exploited by the Roman invaders and several Roman cities were established on, or close to, the site of abandoned Iron Age *oppida*.

Rome and Roman influence was felt in Britain many decades before a legionary ever set foot on British soil. Between 150 BC and 55 BC, Roman amphorae begin appearing on hill fort sites in Hampshire and around the Solent. By the late first century and the period of Julius Caesar's expeditions to Britain, amphorae are instead found further east, in Kent and Essex. Writing around this time, the Roman writer Strabo lists Britain's exports as 'grain, cattle, gold, silver and iron ... also hides and slaves and dogs that are by nature suited to the purposes of the chase'. In return for these commodities, the British tribes of the south took delivery of amphorae full of Roman wine and sets of Roman dinner plates. Hengistbury Head, overlooking Christchurch harbour, seems to have been an important *entrepôt* early on, a place where slaves and grain and wolfhounds were assembled before being shipped across the Channel by Gallic boat-owners. Fig seeds and unworked examples of yellow and purple glass found at the port tell us that other exotic goods were also being brought across for resale to the tribes. Might these new expensive imports have something to do with the rise of the powerful chiefdoms faced by Caesar's armies? Like bronze before it, Roman produce could only be afforded by the wealthy and marked those families out as a distinct elite. Exotic goods served as gifts to loyal war bands, and chiefs giving greater gifts could command ever larger war bands. Status and power, perhaps driven by the exotic produce arriving from Gaul, became important factors in the new tribal system.

It was said that the Britons resembled their Gaulish neighbours very closely, and so there are many details of life and society recorded by Roman writers like Julius Caesar and Tacitus that shed light on Late Iron Age Britain. Caesar

Dating from the early first century BC, this type of pottery was originally manufactured in Armorica, northern France, before being imported into southern Britain. (*A. Wilkins*)

makes a clear distinction between the wealthy noble families and the common poor. He states that the common man is bound in service to members of the aristocracy in an almost feudal manner.

A chief could expect certain obligations from the poorer families bound to him, and he in return had certain duties and responsibilities. Ties to other clans and tribes could be maintained through marriage, as in other cultures, but also through the fostering of sons who were brought up by their adoptive parents until manhood. Such ties were needed, because both Gauls and Britons were known to be boastful, warlike, and eager for battle. Too often this martial ardour was directed at a neighbouring tribe, with the result that long running feuds could develop. Tacitus remarks:

> Now they are distracted between the warring factions of rival chiefs. Indeed nothing has helped [the Romans] more in fighting against this powerful nation [of Britain] than their ability to co-operate. It is but seldom that two or three states unite to repel a common danger; thus, fighting in separate groups, all are conquered.

Accounts of the Roman conquest of Britain bear this out. Prior to Caesar's first expedition in 55 BC, the chief of the Catuvellauni, a man called Cassivellaunus, had been in a continual state of war with the other tribes and had even defeated his neighbours, the Trinovantes, forcing them to submit to him. No doubt because of Cassivellaunus's talent for warfare, the British tribes had elected him as their commander-in-chief for their campaign against the Romans. Caesar soon left Britain, to be murdered in Rome a decade later, but when the legions returned again in AD 43, the main force marched straight for the Catuvellauni homeland. This was where the centre of power in Late Iron Age Britain lay, where the most pugnacious warlords hounded their neighbours. It was also the region where most of the 'Dressel 1B' Roman amphora were found—imports of luxury wine from the continent that could be dated to around the time of Cassivellaunus.

With the British tribes unable or unwilling to work together, hill forts were defeated piecemeal across southern England. Tribes further north, like the Brigantes and Parisi, remained pro-Roman—for as long as they could. Inevitably, the legions were drawn northward and when the giant confederation of the Brigantes suffered a change of ruler, a war of pacification in the north finally led to the end of a free Britain south of the Solway-Tyne frontier. The Scottish tribes, hidden away in their highland territories, proved tougher to conquer; the final attempt being left half finished by the sick emperor Septimius Severus in AD 211. Henceforth Hadrian's Wall, constructed a century earlier, would mark out the edge of Rome's most westerly frontier: Britannia.

2

SURVIVAL IN THE MESOLITHIC

Only when I am sleeping I am not a hunter. I am a hunter all the time I am awake. That is what I am and who I am. I kill animals for meat.

Gonga, a Hadza tribesman

Rising out of the morning mists across the lake rose the sun, burning orange like an ember on the camp fire. As if to herald its coming the birds of the forest had erupted into song, but as the sun rose higher into the pale sky, their cries began to slowly subside. Nothing moved, there was no sound. Shadowy forest lined the lakeside as far as the eye could follow.

Suddenly the flat calm of the vast lake was broken. A grey heron, silent and majestic, lifted clear of its perch within a reed bed. It swept low over the water with broad wings beating, and its long legs trailing behind. Ripples spread out from the reed bed.

Something had disturbed the heron, and the two brothers watched carefully for signs of movement. Yes, now they could see the elk drinking from the lake, but well hidden within the reeds. The elk had been cornered two days ago and shot with arrows, but he was strong and would take several days to die. The hunters were desperate not to lose him, for the meat of the beast would feed their families for a week or more. The men moved quickly along the edge of the birch woods with the intention of cutting of the elk's path of retreat from the shore.

Perhaps of all the periods of British history, the Mesolithic is the most entrancing and also the most enigmatic. However, it is also relatively unknown to the layman, who may recognise the mammoth hunters of the Ice Age, and the technological wizardry of the early Stonehenge builders, but not realise that there is a vast gulf of human prehistory that separates them—something like 4,000 years or the equivalent of 160 human generations. Of the entire human occupation in the British Isles, from the time the glaciers of the Ice Age retreated up until today, the Mesolithic takes up an extraordinary two-fifths.

At its start, as the ice retreated and the frozen wastes from the Cotswolds to the Cairngorms began to give way to forest, human hunters and their families moved in to prey upon the forest animals. The Mesolithic communities became part of the natural world, unlike their descendants, who would simply exploit it. Without towns or villages, metal tools, agriculture, writing, beasts of burden, or formal government, the families and clans of Britain lived out those 160 generations, moving through the forest, hunting deer and wild cattle, gathering berries, herbs and nuts, camping, and then moving on. This way of life sustained the human population and left few discernible marks on the natural environment.

The Lost Lake

In some places the Mesolithic hunters did leave behind some evidence of their lives, though that evidence is often slight. One place is Star Carr, North Yorkshire, a Mesolithic encampment that sat on the shores of a large lake in the wide Vale of Pickering. The lake was formed from water melted out of the retreating Ice Age glaciers, but today it is lost, along with the birch wood forests that surrounded it. Today a modern field system sliced by drainage ditches stands as mute testimony to the forgotten lake of the Mesolithic.

Excavations conducted in 1949–51 revealed a well-preserved bed of branches and brushwood that extended out from the shore into the reed bed. This platform was associated with flint-knapping and the working of antler and the flint was taken from the nearby Yorkshire Wolds as well as the beaches of Flamborough Head. Scatters of flint were found around the lake shore and also on several small islands. Of course, if people were living on islands this implies that they had the skills to build their own boats, and Clark's team discovered a wooden paddle. No boats have yet been found, but it is likely that the hunters built either cow skin coracles or canoes dug out of logs.

Thirty years later a more substantial timber platform was discovered to the east of Clark's brushwood camp and more recent work has extended the Mesolithic presence all along the shoreline and further back on the tree-lined slopes overlooking the lake. Yet, although finds have been recovered from sites around the lake edge as well as the islands, no other site in the area resembles Star Carr. Compare the 192 barbed hunting points found at Star Carr to only two other examples found elsewhere around the lake. Few of the animal bones found at the site were from meaty joints, those more edible parts were cut free and taken elsewhere to be eaten. If the platform at Star Carr was not a typical hunting camp, what was it?

Clues come from a collection of deer antlers found by Clark that were

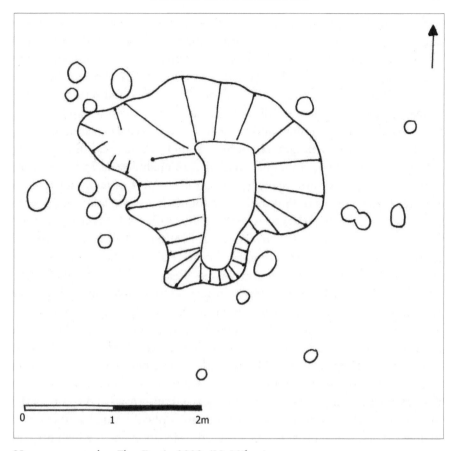

House excavated at Flag Fen in 2008. (*N. Milner*)

probably used as ritual head-dresses. Did shamans carry out hunting rituals on the platform? In the later Neolithic and Bronze Ages, wooden platforms were commonly used by native Britons to cast offerings into sacred waters. It is possible that the Star Carr camp was actually a sacred site, a meeting point where religious ceremonies could be performed and craft activities carried out. If so, it would have acted as a central point for the tribe who hunted and fished at the lake.

Star Carr remains one of the most famous and most important Mesolithic sites in Europe. Current theory suggests that it was a winter site, a lowland base camp used by bands of nomadic hunter-gatherers. Here, in hide tents erected on the brushwood floor, several families could live together, hunting deer and other animals in the forests and restocking supplies of harpoons and points. Fishing was undoubtedly practiced, although fish bones have not survived. In the summer these families moved north onto the North Yorkshire Moors (at that time heavily forested), where many scatters of worked flint have been found. Other hunters moved up into the Pennine Mountains where over 540 sites of worked flint have been recorded, many associated with camps and hearths. The Pennines may not have been forested at the time Star Carr was in use, instead they were open heaths with a scattering of hazel trees. The tribes followed game up into these highlands in the summer and returned to the beaches, lakes, and valleys in winter to fish and eat up the stores of hazelnuts that were gathered in autumn during the final deer hunting expeditions.

We know that hunter-gatherers moved from lowland areas in the winter where they carried out communal activities, to upland areas in the summer where they dispersed into smaller groups. It is a feature of many subsistence cultures today. Studies of flint tools have found that the upland camps were places where hunting points were made, while other tools, such as scrapers, were used in the winter camps to prepare animal skins. Although the families moved according to a seasonal round, they were also flexible and could alter their plans and use alternate resources and alternate camp sites. Should the band head up the river to catch brown trout? Or to the moorland where deer were more easily tracked? What about heading to Bridlington Bay where abundant shellfish could be collected? Each decision was weighted with important considerations of time, effort, and return. Deer supplied a great deal of meat, along with hide, bone, antler, and sinew—however, hunting deer was risky and several weeks may pass without a sure kill. Tracks may be missed, wounded deer may escape, or may avoid the arrows and spears of the hunters altogether. Contrast this with the surety of collecting hawthorn and juniper berries, which provide much needed sustenance, but at a high price in time and energy devoted to collecting and processing.

It is likely that every hunter-gatherer band moved between at least three separate locales within the year, and probably more. At each site there would be a number of resources to exploit from a number of well-known and well-used camp sites. Tent poles, hearths, and wooden cooking tripods could all be left in situ until the hunters returned, or could be left behind for the benefit of others. Canadian tribes in the eighteenth and nineteenth centuries considered such a practice bad luck, however, and always dismantled their camps. Perhaps the Star Carr hunters did the same.

Steven Mithen believes that the basic unit of Mesolithic society was the family, and that families lived together for a large part of the year (most likely the winter months) in communities of up to 100 individuals. This 'band' may have had contact with others in the region, establishing a social network spanning hundreds of kilometres. It is highly likely that families or bands moved from one region to another, travelling great distances on foot and engaging in trade and social relations with other bands.

From ethnographic studies, it is likely these hunting bands were probably egalitarian, without a dominant chief. Yet the uneven spread of resources across Europe meant that some bands had access to more than their neighbours. Hunting bands may well have had different levels of 'wealth', there were no rich individuals, but there were certainly groups who had more status, due to rich hunting grounds or trade links for exotic materials.

Tools and Technology

Popular images of Stone Age folk are dominated by brutish men and women clad in the skins of wild animals. Certainly the Mesolithic hunter-gatherers relied upon the animals they hunted for the raw materials of clothing, but it wasn't until the well-preserved remains of Ötzi the Ice Man were discovered in 1991 that archaeologists realised just how sophisticated the achievements of these people were.

This traveller, hiking through the Alps around 3300 BC, was killed by assailants and his body preserved by the cold, covered by winter snowfall and then frozen in the glacial ice. Although he dates from a much later period, his clothing follows the Mesolithic tradition of using only grasses and animal skins, rather than textiles. Yet Ötzi's clothing was designed and constructed with considerable skill, he did not wear a slap-dash covering of deerskins, but a carefully constructed set of clothes designed to protect him from the chilly Alpine weather.

Ötzi wore a tunic, loincloth, and leggings all of goatskin, a long calf-skin belt, a cap of bear fur, shoes made from a variety of animal hides, and a woven grass cape. With so many deer appearing on the Star Carr menu, it is likely that the hunter's tunic, loincloth, and leggings would be of deerskin. The tunic was not elaborate, it may have been as simple as a rectangle wrapped around the body, held in place with a strap over the shoulder and the wide leather belt at the waist, or it may have had sleeves. Sleeved garments are known from the Bronze Age, but that is still over 7,000 years in the future.

The goatskin leggings were crucial to an Alpine man like Ötzi, and may have been used during the winters of Mesolithic Britain. They were, essentially, tubes of goatskin pulled over each leg with laces at the top and bottom that allowed them to be tied to shoe and belt, preventing them from 'riding up'.

Although the Ice Man's shoes were of a complex design, Mesolithic shoes were very likely much simpler affairs. Some of the oldest Neolithic shoe designs were simply an oval of deerskin with slits around the edge. The shoe was bound to the foot by threading a lace through the slits and pulling it tight, and around the instep by another lace passing under the shoe. A prehistoric example of this design is the Schindejoch shoe, found in the Netherlands, but this simple shoe design also survived into the historical period. The Drumacoon 'bag shoe' was found in an Irish peat bog and dates to the early Medieval period. Another version, surviving on the west coast of Ireland into the nineteenth century, was the 'pampootie'—a traditional skin shoe with the fur left on the outside. Ötzi's shoes had an upper part made of bearskin, but like the pampootie, the fur was left on the outside.

The author has made himself a pair of shoes that follow this basic design, using red deer skin, with the hair on the outside, and a with a lace of goatskin. They were very comfortable, and weathered soft snow very well, the hairs providing much needed grip while walking. Rain or wet grass proved to be a serious weakness, however, and the shoes were quickly soaked. The simple method of binding without fine stitching meant that the shoes were far from waterproof, but that may have been a factor that prehistoric men and women were happy to cope with. Protection from stones, thorns and twigs may instead have motivated the hunters to fashion shoes for themselves.

It might seem that these clothes were nothing more than crude animal skins, yet they required cleaning, tanning, and stitching. Marks made by flint scrapers were found on the inside of Ötzi's tunic, and chemical analysis shows that the skins were tanned with animal fat and wood smoke. Each goatskin panel was stitched to its neighbour with twisted sinew in a cross-stitch technique. Protection from the British weather may have come from a grass cape, similar to the one found with the Ice Man, or from a hide cloak that could have been made waterproof by smearing with animal fat, as peasants are known to have done in the Roman Empire.

Perhaps the most interesting part of Ötzi's clothing was his calfskin belt, long enough to wrap around his waist twice, and with an integral sewn-in pouch. This little pouch, tucked beneath his tunic and capable of being laced shut, contained his most important items—his survival kit. Here he carried tinder fungus used for lighting fires, a bone awl used in leatherwork, and three flint tools (a scraper, a drill, and a flint blade).

With these essentials, a Mesolithic hunter could skin an animal, clean its hide, and turn it into clothing or other useful objects. Like many traditional groups, the people of the Mesolithic would have travelled lightly, carrying only what they needed to live off the land. Of maximum importance are tools made of flint, a stone that cannot be relied upon to be at hand when it is needed. With flint, a huge number of practical tools could be made and tiny blades (microliths) could be fashioned and fixed to spear-points. Almost every other tool was taken from the forest or from the animals brought down on the hunt.

What else might the Star Carr families be expected to carry with them? We have already mentioned tinder fungus, but nodules of iron pyrite might also be gathered from local beaches. Struck with a sharp flint, these pyrites send sparks into the fungus, which can cause it to smoulder. The heat is enough to set alight a handful of dry grasses. The nomadic Evenk people of Siberia carry embers from the morning fire with them on a trek, using it to start their evening camp fire. They do this by placing a glowing ember into a small birch bark pot filled with green leaves. A pot just like this was found with Ötzi.

A knife is essential for survival even today; it is a versatile tool and in the Mesolithic was fashioned from flint and mounted in a handle with glue-like birch resin. Ötzi's flint dagger had an ash-wood handle and he had made a scabbard for it from woven bark fibre. Most likely he made the dagger, as well as his other tools, himself. The Star Carr hunters were likewise equally self-reliant. Ötzi carried another important tool with which he fashioned other tools. It was a pressure flaker, a fire-hardened point of deer antler embedded in a handle of lime wood. Pressure flakers are used in flint knapping to create a good cutting edge on a flint blade, and to alter the shape of the flake to suit a particular need. With a pebble and a pressure flaker, any hunter could reliably fashion new scrapers, blades, and microliths.

The microliths were quickly worked to become razor-sharp arrowheads. They provided a nasty cutting edge and were bound onto arrow shafts with birch resin. Although no bows were found at the lakeside, bows from the later Neolithic have been discovered at Holmegaard and Ringkloster (Denmark), Edington Burtle (England), and elsewhere. They are a type known as a stave or flat bow, tillered from a single piece of elm or yew, and capable of considerable penetrative power. Every hunter at Lake Flixton would also have owned a spear, tipped with a flint flake and fastened with fibre cord and pine resin.

The Business of Hunting

If modern ethnographic studies can be used as a comparison, hunting will have been an exclusively male preserve, while the women raised children, tended camp, and gathered berries, nuts, and roots. Most of these food products required some form of processing before they were edible, and different foodstuffs required more or less labour to achieve this.

What was available around the banks of Lake Flixton? The tribe was certainly able to collect birds' eggs. Water birds like stork, heron, goose, moorhen, and whooper swan will have nested in the reed beds around the lake and the nests would have been quite accessible. If Star Carr was indeed a winter camp, then the tribe will have been able to catch ducks and collect duck eggs. Hornsea Mere, a shallow glacial lake of the same proportions as Lake Flixton laying some 40 km away, is still an annual destination for thousands of ducks from breeding grounds all over Europe. These include mallard, teal, and widgeon in the shallows and diving ducks such as pochard, goldeneye, and tufted duck. Working together, with boys beating the reeds with sticks, ducks could be flushed toward hunters who held out nets woven out of nettle fibre. In a world without cookpots, the duck eggs could be eaten by knocking a hole in the top and left in embers to cook in their own 'pot'. I have found this a great way to cook eggs in the hearth, with care needed not to let the egg tip over. Eggs can also be wrapped in moss and left to 'steam' until hardboiled. Birds provided feathers, fat, oil, and skin—at Star Carr, a bead was found made from a bird bone.

In the reeds themselves, a grub over 2 cm long can be found, which is large enough to have been worth collecting. Insects and grubs are still a source of nutrition for some tribes today. Other lakeside food sources included toads, crayfish, and freshwater mussels. Knowledge must have been passed down about these food sources; glands behind the toad's eyes, for example, are poisonous.

Meat was obtained from the great range of mammals that populated the vast Mesolithic forests of Britain. These included red and roe deer, wild boar, elk, and auroch. Aurochs were made extinct in the seventeenth century and were a species of giant wild cattle. There were plenty of other mammals, too; some were killed for their skins, bones, or teeth, while others might have been killed in self-defence. Some, like red fox, wild cat, badger, stoat, and weasel, are still found in British woodlands (and were probably snared by Mesolithic hunters). Others, like lynx, wolf, bear, and beaver, were made extinct long ago and are now found only on the European mainland. Only one animal had been successfully domesticated—the dog (a descendant of the grey wolf), which was almost certainly used in hunting. Wild boar are still hunted with dogs in some parts of the world today. The dogs bring the boar to bay giving the hunter time to catch up and then dispatch the wild pig himself. Boars were prized by hunters throughout prehistory, probably for their fat, which proved to be valuable energy source in such an active and mobile society.

The business of hunting also involves the building and setting of traps and in the Mesolithic these would have employed pliant saplings, and nooses and snares made of cord. Much smaller prey were probably hunted and trapped by the boys of the tribe, as happens today within tribes like the Hadza in Tanzania. Dormice, red squirrels, hedgehogs, small birds, shrew, and voles would all have made easy snacks for hunters or their sons, but unfortunately there is almost no record of these creatures on Mesolithic sites. Aside from the wooden paddle and the 191 beautifully carved antler harpoon heads, neither is there much hard evidence for fishing at Star Carr, yet fish must have formed an important part of Mesolithic diet, particularly at a lakeside settlement like Star Carr. Fish traps made of willow branches are known from some Mesolithic sites, but barbed harpoons, nets, and canoes would all have aided the fisherman. Rolls of birch bark were found at the Lake Flixton site, and these may well have been the floats for fishing nets; similar fishing floats were used by Scandinavian fishermen until recently.

One tradition that is common to many hunters from tribal societies is the removal, and eating, of the animal's liver. Cooked quickly in the embers of a fire it provides instant sustenance for the exhausted hunters. It is tempting to picture the Star Carr hunters celebrating a kill in this way. Once the animal had been carried back to the settlement, it required butchering and, of course, nothing was wasted. The hunter brought to his tribe food, skins for clothing and shoes, antler for harpoon heads and mattocks, bone for awls and needles, and sinew for use as thread, bowstrings, and snares.

In camp the carcass would have been bled to ensure the meat would keep, this also purged the meat of its strong taste. Blood would probably have been caught and drunk, as happens in some modern hunting cultures. Next, the animal was skinned. The hide of the wild pig, however, holds a lot of fat, forcing the hunters to scald or burn off the hair, before beginning the butchery. Flint tools were used to butcher the carcass, as tell-tale cut marks on surviving Mesolithic bone show. The placement of these marks indicate that the hunters butchered animals in much the same way as we do today, this is a skill to be learnt, with weak points exploited by flint blades and muscle power.

Nicky Milner, who has directed excavations at Star Carr, suggested that the meat of a large animal, such as a red deer, auroch, or elk, might be smoked or dried in order to preserve as much of the meat as possible for later consumption. A simple wooden rack or platform built over hot embers could have served as a method for smoking strips of meat, and a pile of leaves from a hardwood tree dumped onto the embers would have provided the preserving smoke.

The Business of Gathering

Skill and knowledge of the natural world were both key to Mesolithic survival. It was not simply a matter of being 'lucky on the hunt', but of understanding where food was and how it could be most efficiently gathered. Survival often meant weighing up how much energy needed to be expended to collect and process a foodstuff against how much energy (how many calories) that food would ultimately provide. Digging up the edible roots of a plant might well provide a hearty meal, if done at the right time of the year, but done out of season, the digger would go hungry and would have expended costly physical effort with no return. Knowledge of life cycles—of trees, plants, and animals— held the secret to successful gathering. Of course not all plants in Britain can be eaten and several species are actually poisonous. Skill was needed not just to know which was which, but also which part of a plant might cause harm. Cuckoopint, for example, has an edible root that is harmful if not cooked; the rest of the plant is also poisonous. Likewise, the leaves of nettles are notorious for their painful sting, but once boiled in water they become edible.

Nuts are an obvious Mesolithic food source, and hazelnuts seem to have been especially popular. Piles of charred hazelnut shells have been found at many sites from this period, including an excavated campsite on the Scottish island of Colonsay. Although nuts are not easy to digest without cooking, they are rich in protein and packed with calories.

The green leaves of many plants are also edible, but will become bitter once the plant begins to flower. One way that Mesolithic gatherers might have extended the use of a resource like this would have been to cut back any new shoots, promoting the growth of new and more succulent leaves. Other parts of the plant, such as seeds or the tips of new shoots, can also be harvested. Mesolithic sites across northern Europe have yielded many finds of water lily seeds, which must have been eaten by hunter-gatherers at Star Carr and elsewhere. Seeds, although easily gathered, require a good deal of processing in order to make them palatable. Typically, seeds are parched or toasted, and then ground into a flour ready for cooking. It is the exploitation of grass seeds that ultimately led to the practice of agriculture.

In Britain there are almost a hundred species of edible roots and these will have provided the tribes with a source of energy-rich carbohydrates. Those plants with edible roots provide a valuable resource that can often be exploited throughout the year unlike, of course, leaves, seeds, and nuts. However, these perennial roots often lose their above-ground parts at certain times of the year and so local knowledge would have been needed to find the buried roots. Some of the roots are produced by biennial plants, whose life cycle is spread over the course of two years. If the roots aren't dug up in the first year, then the root becomes worthless, since all of the goodness being stored there is used by the plant to grow its second-year shoots and flowers.

Edible roots often need very little work to turn them into a meal and they can easily be dried and stored for long periods of time. In this way, like smoked and dried meat, they allowed hunter-gatherer groups to retain a stock of foodstuffs for the leaner months of the year.

Cooking for the Tribe

In a world without cook pots, one could imagine that the only way meat could be cooked was for it to be spit roasted over an open fire. Likewise, we can imagine that green leaves gathered in the Mesolithic might simply be eaten raw. But, although direct evidence for the Mesolithic is lacking, similar societies today prepare their foods in a wide variety of ways.

Let us look at meat, for example. Spit roasting was almost certainly used for some animals, but would not be suitable for all. It is quite an intensive and time consuming method of cookery and other ways of dealing with meat were almost certainly used. My favourite is the earth oven, which we discuss at length later in the book. Here, a pit is lined with stones and a fire burnt on top of them; once the stones are hot, joints of meat are added to the pit and soil is placed on top. Heat from the stones cooks the meat over a period of several hours. Alternatively, river clay allows the cook to cover food with clay, and after it has dried, place it into the embers of a fire. Now the heat radiates inwards, through the clay, and cooks the meat within and preventing its juices from escaping. This and other cooking techniques will be explained in much greater depth later on.

From a modern perspective, it is easy to assume that 'gathering' simply involves picking fruits, nuts, and berries of off trees and bushes. Unfortunately, man cannot live by fruits and berries alone—in Mesolithic Britain, such a food resource is dependent on the season and would never have been abundant enough to feed several large families in one location.

While many wild plants can be eaten raw, there are many that require processing in order to render them palatable. Hazelnuts, for example, are best eaten once roasted; this improves the flavour, makes them easier to digest, and helps to preserve them for later consumption. Berries, like sloe and bird cherry, require pulverizing between two stones and then drying as simple cakes in the sun. Root foods such as sea beet, sea kale, goat's-beard, and pig nut can be eaten raw, but once roasted they are softer, easier to eat, and often tastier. Some resources require almost as much processing as wheat—the seeds of Fat Hen, for example, must be stripped from the stem, dried in the sun, rubbed to break them from their seed cases, lightly parched on a hot stone, and then ground into flour. This flour would be baked as bush bread, something known to modern Australians as a 'damper', a flat-bread composed simply of flour and water and baked on the ashes of a campfire. Seeds of the ribwort plantain, as well as several other species, can likewise make decent flat-breads.

There are some plant resources that require even more complex processing than this. Yellow waterlily seeds have survived on some Mesolithic sites (particularly in Denmark), but the seed-bearing fruits must first be gathered by coracle or dug-out canoe. Back on dry land they are left to rot in vats of water and once the seeds are free they are then rinsed and dried. Like the seeds of Fat Hen, they must then have their outer coverings removed, then winnowed, parched by the fire, and finally ground into flour.

Many of these techniques, used by hunter-gatherer societies today and by Mesolithic groups in the past, are identical to the processing of wheat grains in arable farming. The leap from gathering to harvesting was not a leap of imagination across a vast gulf of knowledge. The shift to sedentary agriculture required many of the skills that Mesolithic communities already possessed.

Did the families at Star Carr, huddled around flickering campfires, enjoy the lives they led? Or were they merely surviving? Anthropologists who have followed modern nomadic groups have discovered that they certainly enjoy more free time than their crop-farming cousins. In leaner times of course, the Star Carr community may have struggled to feed everyone. It was the lingering threat of famine and bad winters set against the backdrop of an expanding Mesolithic population that made agriculture, when it arrived on the shores of Britain, so attractive.

3

FARMING THE LAND

The most ancient farmers determined many of the practices by experiment, their descendants for the most part by imitation. We ought to do both—imitate others and attempt by experiment to do some things in a different way.

Varro, *Re Rustica*

Initially, this book was to look at food and cookery in prehistoric Britain, but it is impossible to discuss food without looking at its origins. Where was it grown? How was it grown? Could it be stored? How were animals controlled and used? Today, farming and food are almost completely divorced from one another, with consumers dropping sliced loaves, tins, and shrink-wrapped meat into their baskets, often oblivious to the methods used to grow or rear it.

Of course, in prehistory, there really was no such thing as a consumer—this is an invention of industrialisation and free market economics. Our ancestors, on the other hand, consumed what they produced, more or less, and used exchange and gift-giving to obtain items (like metal, jewellery, or colourful dyes) that they could not source for themselves. Only a tiny elite existed at any one time in British prehistory, a small number of wealthy families that were able to survive off the toil of others. For the simple farming family, the preparation of every meal was actually the end point of a long process that began at least a year earlier. While the modern householder might plan a meal a couple of days, or perhaps a week, in advance, the prehistoric farmer was forced to work to a much longer timescale.

For the earliest communities at the start of the Neolithic, an even greater task faced them. There simply was no farmland, either for the cultivation of wheat and barley or for the grazing of cattle. Land had to be cleared and, as populations rose steadily throughout the Neolithic and into the Bronze Age, ever more land was required for agriculture.

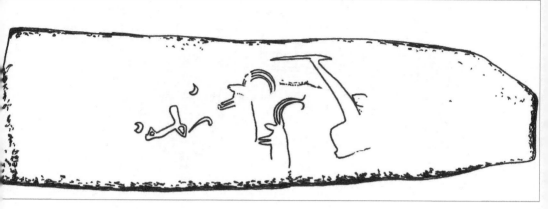

Part of a standing stone from Gavrinis, Brittany; carved into its surface are emblems of the agricultural lifestyle: ard, ox, sheep, sickle, and axe. (*C. T. Le Roux*)

At the start of the Neolithic, much of Britain was covered in forest. Small plots of land, opened up by the felling of trees with stone axes, must have been sufficient for the needs of the small number of farming communities at that time. The needs were simple: the farmers wanted to hoard foodstuffs to see them through the winter. In Britain, natural food supplies are drastically curtailed for up to nine months of the year. A plant was needed that produced food annually that was amenable to storage for a full year. Nut trees take several years to mature, for example, and do not bear edible nuts every year. Early farmers in the Near East settled on wild einkorn grass (*Triticum monococcoides*), a primitive cereal whose seeds (it must have been noticed) were slightly larger than those of other grasses. We know that the seeds of several wild plants were probably ground up by Mesolithic gatherers in order to make flour. Wheat grass would have been processed in just the same way and under cultivation some of the seeds were put aside for replanting.

Where seed beds were needed, trees had to be felled first. The investment in labour to clear land and to grow these new crops quickly led to more permanent or semi-permanent settlements. Crops of emmer wheat (*Triticum dioccum*) and barley (*Hordeum spontaneum*) began to be planted across Britain. Population levels rose as families needed more manpower with which to maintain the crops, and more hungry mouths required ever greater land clearances. Pollen and snail shell analysis from Dorset and Wiltshire indicate that in this particular corner of Britain enough trees had been felled by 3200 BC that the landscape was now open grassland, with some areas of farmland and scrub 'regrowth'.

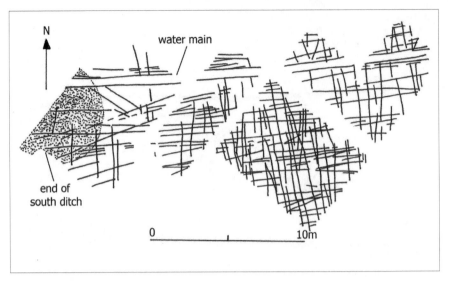

Marks cut by prehistoric ards that were discovered under, and adjacent to, the South Street long barrow, Wiltshire. They date to around 2000 BC. (*J. G. Evans*)

Field Systems

We know that fields existed and were properly demarcated. Some large earthen burial mounds were constructed over (and so preserved) traces of farmland. Beneath South Street Long Barrow, near Avebury, archaeologists discovered furrows cut by ards (the earliest form of simple plough). Fences, ditches, and planted hedges were used to mark out some of these individual fields in order to prevent cattle, pigs, and other farm animals from eating the crops growing in them. Examples of these kinds of Neolithic field boundaries are few in number, but some have been identified at Rougham Hill in County Clare, Fengate in eastern England, and on the Shetland Islands. Evidence for cattle droveways has also been found at Fengate and at Hambledon Hill, Dorset, where two cross dykes have been interpreted as routes by cattle to reach new pasture.

It was not until the Early Bronze Age, when Stonehenge was at its peak of development, that elaborate and large scale field systems begin to appear in the archaeological record. These systems were made up of small fields arranged together in groups. Field boundaries may initially have been formed as a strip of uncleared ground between two plots of farmland, on this strip of land hedges, brambles and thorn bushes flourished and soon acted as a natural barrier. Hedge laying practices carried out by prehistoric farmers would turn these tangles of stem and bush into a tough, stock-proof barrier. Other boundaries were formed by earthen banks, or from the practice of picking stones off the land and dumping them into cairns along the field edge. On Dartmoor these cairns were sometimes used by farmers as repositories for the ashes of their dead. Stones certainly need to be cleared before crops are sown and even before animals are grazed, but constant maintenance is needed since stones have a tendency to keep appearing at the surface during cultivation.

Some field systems, like the Dartmoor 'reaves', were subdivided by low, purpose-built, drystone walls. Similarly, sarsen stones were used to construct drystone field boundaries on Fyfield Down, Wiltshire. Some of these sarsens were cracked and burnt, suggesting the use of fire to break apart the larger sarsens into more manageable chunks. The Fyfield Down walls acted as revetments to the accumulation of plough soil that naturally migrated downslope each year. These banks of earth that built up downslope over time are known as lynchets, and they create very visible terracing on a hillside. Some of the known Bronze Age field systems extend over large areas, and one of the most extensive on Dartmoor covers an area of 900 hectares.

The size of individual Bronze and Iron Age fields is small in comparison with fields laid out using modern farming techniques. It seems likely that a

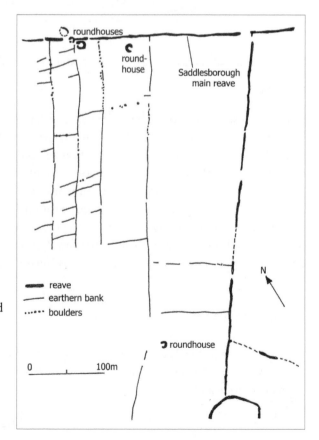

Reaves (or stone and earth banks) on Shaugh Moor, Dartmoor, in Devon. Reaves were used to parcel-up farmland in the south-west; here on Shaugh Moor, the western section was further subdivided, and then divided again into even smaller plots.
(*J. Collis*)

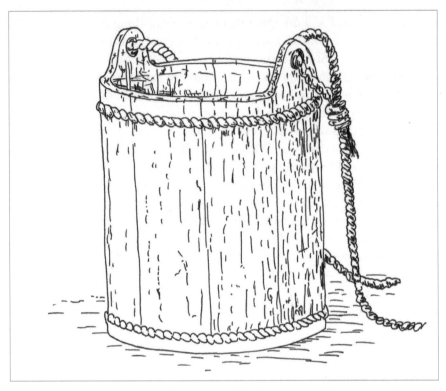

Wooden bucket of Bronze Age date, from Wilsford Down, Wiltshire. (*L. Coleman*)

single demarcated field was able to be harvested, ploughed, seeded, or weeded by a single family in a single day. In many parts of Britain, small clusters of fields, forming a 'farmstead' system that related to a single settlement or roundhouse, seem to have been the norm. Fields discovered in prehistoric Britain are generally rectangular in shape and 0.7 hectares or less in area. Typically, the dimensions of these fields are around 70 × 50 m. They are rarely located far from a roundhouse and the evidence suggests that the fields a family tended were usually close to the family home. Cattle required more distant pasture, as well as a network of ditch-lined droveways to reach them.

Arable Farming

For here now is the Age of Iron. Never by daytime will there be an end to hard work and pain, nor in the night to weariness, when the gods will send anxieties to trouble us.

Hesiod, *Works and Days*

From the Bronze Age into the Iron Age and beyond, bread has provided British households with their staple food. Much of the arable farming that took place in prehistory concerned the production of wheat, barley, and oats—cereal crops that formed the mainstay of the diet. Crop farming requires the careful management of fields, fields that first must be created, manured and maintained, seeds that must be planted, crops that must be carefully managed, and then harvested, with some of the seed corn going into storage for next year's sowing. The story does not stop there. A good deal of processing is required to turn sheaves of wheat into flour ready for mixing into dough at the fireside.

All arable farming begins with the tilling the ground, breaking up hard-packed earth into a loose soil that will be ready to accept a scatter of seeds. The modern plough is an innovative machine carrying out several operations at once. A knife-like blade, called a coulter, sits at the front of the plough and cuts into the soil just ahead of the main blade or share. The share then turns the soil over and a curved mouldboard further back flips the soil upside down to one side of the shallow furrow. In this way fresh nutrients are brought to the surface while weeds and the remains of stubble and earlier crops are buried. Prior to the ploughs of the Roman period, however, only some of these technical innovations had been recognized.

In 1944, a well-preserved Bronze Age plough was discovered at Donneruplund, Denmark, and others have been unearthed at Dostrup and Hendriksmose. Since it lacked a mouldboard with which it turned over the soil, the Donneruplund plough was actually an ard.

Ards are still used today in poorer farming areas. The ard cuts into the earth with an angled wooden spike and creates only a narrow furrow called a 'drill', which leaves the intervening ground undisturbed. Traces of this implement have been found across Britain as ard marks like those beneath South Street long barrow. Well-preserved ard marks have also been found gouged into the chalk bedrock on Slonk Hill, near Brighton, and at other locations across Britain. To further break up the soil within the field, the ard was often used to cross-plough at 90 degrees. Lacking the sophistication and utility of the later mouldboard plough, the ard was redesigned and variations of the tool came into being, each suited to a different kind of job.

Where the soil was heavy or as-yet uncultivated, a rip ard (also known as a 'sod buster') was employed, its sharply angled spike digging in deep and stubbornly locking in place every 2 or 3 metres. For cutting furrows in previously cultivated land, a bow ard was used. The Donneruplund ard was of this type, fitted with a heart-shaped undershare that lifted the soil and helped churn it up as the ard passed through. Modern trials with a replica of the Donneruplund ard were quite successful, but indicated that the wooden share quickly wore away. Although none was found with the Donneruplund example, iron sleeves to protect the wooden share have been found across Iron Age Europe. In earlier periods, stone points were fitted to the business end of ards in an effort to increase the wear time of these tools. The third type of ard was the seed-furrow ard, used to create particularly narrow drills within previously prepared soil, drills that allowed seed to be sown and crops to be grown in distinct rows that later allowed the farmer to hoe out any weeds growing between them. All of the ards seem to have been pulled by cattle; rock carvings like those from Litsleby in Denmark and Val Camonic in Italy both depict a pair of oxen hauling ards under the direction of a ploughman. Both ploughmen are carrying goads with which to drive the animals on, and in the Val Camonic carving, two associates carry hoes or mattocks with which to break up any stubborn clods of earth left by the ard. Experimental work at Butser Ancient Farm has shown that an experienced ploughman and a well-trained team of oxen can plough half a hectare in a day.

The Roman naturalist Pliny, who died during the eruption of Mount Vesuvius in AD 79, advised Roman farmers to plough their fields several times, and sensible Celtic agriculturalists will have done the same.

> After the furrows have been gone over again transversely, the clods are broken, where there is a necessity for it, with either the harrow or the rake; and this operation is repeated after the seed has been put in. This last harrowing is done, where the usage of the locality will allow of it, with either a toothed harrow, or else a plank attached to the plough.

Pliny, *The Natural World*, 18.49

The preparation of fields ready for planting must also have included manuring. This is the art of artificially adding nutrients to a field from the faeces of domesticated animals and is believed to have begun sometime in the Bronze Age. It is likely that fields were also left fallow for a time, as many were during the Medieval period. In Scotland, poultry and sheep manure was ranked as the most effective, followed by horse and pig manure. Cattle dung was considered the least effective because around three-quarters of its weight is made up of water. To be used it was first mixed with bracken or straw, which tended to soak up its moisture and aid fermentation. Large quantities of the stuff was required since one ton of manure provided only around 5–8 kg of nitrogen and an equally small amount of potassium.

A layer of 'dark earth' found on prehistoric agricultural land at Welland Valley, near Maxey, was made up of manure mixed with domestic rubbish (pieces of bone, pottery, and flint), which may represent hearth sweepings. Was domestic refuse dumped directly onto a manure pile (or 'midden') close to the roundhouse? An ancient tradition found in the farmhouses of Orkney,

The Litsleby rock carving in Denmark depicts a ploughman and his team of oxen. He seems to be using a branch as a goad and is just beginning to plough his third furrow or 'drill'. (*P. V. Glob*)

This rock carving from Val Camonic, in Italy, depicts a team of oxen drawing an ard across a field. One man guides the ard, another leads the oxen, while a third breaks up clods of earth behind the plough. (*P. J. Reynolds*)

Shetland, and Caithness might throw some light on this practice. Here, a hollow next to the house's central hearth was created by the regular scraping of ashes that were pushed off the hearth. In Orkney these ashes were held by a circle of wet peats, but turves could also have been used. These peats, along with the ash, were thrown into the cattle barn or byre to be used as bedding. In this way peat was used for fuel, converted into ashes, and then used as bedding in the byre. Finally, when the byre was cleaned out, the sweepings were spread as fertiliser onto the fields. It was probably via this method that domestic rubbish found its way onto prehistoric fields at places like Welland Valley and Potterne in Dorset. Cattle must also have been left to graze on recently harvested fields, adding more manure directly to the soil while they munched their way through unwanted crop stubble.

Other sources of manure existed, such as bracken or seaweed. Turf could also be cut from grazing areas and mixed with manure that had been cleaned out of the cattle byre. Regularly turned and left to ferment, this midden would create an effective manure for the fields—although our evidence for such a practice only goes back to the Medieval period. Turf is a resource used to feed cattle and not to be squandered lightly, although it has been calculated that an area of turf around 1.5 hectares in size had to be cut in order to build a typical Bronze Age burial mound. Turves used to roof houses in parts of North West Europe (like the reconstructions at Flag Fen, near Peterborough) actually became rich in potash that rose from the household fire. Every few years these turves would be removed and broken up to be added as fertiliser to the fields. The close connection between field fertility and manure illustrates the fine line that existed between arable and pastoral farming and provided a strong justification for mixed farming in the prehistoric period.

Identifying the crops grown in Bronze Age and Iron Age fields can (in part) be done through the analysis of carbonised seed remains that are found on prehistoric sites. Eight types of cereals can be identified from hundreds of charred seeds found across Britain:

Cereals
- Emmer Wheat (*Triticum dioccum*)
- Old-bread Wheat (*Triticum aestivum*)
- Club Wheat (*Triticum compactum*)
- Spelt Wheat (*Triticum spelta*)
- Naked and Hulled Two-row (*Hordeum distichum*)
- Naked and Hulled Six-row Barley (*Hordeum hexastichum*)
- Rye (*Secale cereale*)
- Oats (*Avena*)

Spelt dominates the finds of cereal grains in the Late Iron Age and was without doubt the most popular strain of wheat to be grown prior to the Roman invasion. Pliny talked of a Celtic strain of spelt:

> [It was] peculiar to that country ... a grain of remarkable whiteness. Another difference, again, is the fact that it yields nearly four pounds more of bread to the modius than any other kind of spelt.

Pliny, *Natural History*, 18.11

Prior to the introduction of spelt in the Iron Age, emmer and bread wheat dominated the diets of prehistoric families. Limited evidence for the cultivation of oats comes from Bronze Age sites in North-West Europe where climatic conditions were cold and wet. It is thought that oats were not an important crop in prehistoric Britain.

Legumes
- Peas (*Pisum sativum*)
- Celtic Beans (*Vicia faba minor*)

Seeds from Celtic beans and peas do not survive well. Evidence for pea cultivation comes from an example found at Bronze Age Grimes Graves and another from Iron Age Hengistbury Head. The only beans found in prehistoric contexts is the small Celtic bean ('tic' or 'horse bean') and no other types seem to have been cultivated in this period. Since the legumes fix nitrogen into the soil while cereals extract it, a canny farmer will have learnt to grow legumes in one year, and in the second year sow wheat or barley. Unfortunately, hard evidence for crop rotation does not survive within the archaeological record.

Vegetables
- Turnip (*Brassica rapa*)
- Carrot (*Daucus carota*)
- Fat-Hen (*Chenopodium album*)

There is only one prehistoric record of turnip in Britain, at Bu, in the Orkneys, and that comes from an Iron Age context. Wild carrot is represented in the list, a thin and woody vegetable that was pale or purple in colour. The large edible carrots eaten today originated in the Middle East and arrived in Britain during the later Medieval period. Fat-hen is a weed, pulled up from flowerbeds in gardens across the modern Britain, yet seeds of fat-hen are commonly found on domestic prehistoric sites, outnumbered only by the cereal crops that are listed above. With this in mind, fat-hen was certainly cultivated and eaten prior to the Roman period. Fat-hen leaves are edible and its seeds can be ground up into flour to make bread. Lastly, the whole plant can be dried and fed to animals as winter fodder.

Other Crops
- Flax (*Linum usitatissimum*)
- Woad (*Isatis tinctoria*)
- Gold-of-pleasure (*Camelina sativa*)
- Opium poppy (*Papaver somniferim*)
- Hemp (*Cannabis sativa*)

Other crops were cultivated for uses other than food, and these are likely to have been grown in kitchen plots, adjacent to the roundhouse. Flax was grown both for its fibres and for the oil contained within its seeds.

Pliny the Elder remarked:

> The part [of flax] that lies nearest to the outer coat is known by the name of 'stuppa;' it is a flax of inferior quality, and is mostly employed for making the wicks of lamps... There is a certain amount of skill required in hatchelling flax and dressing it: it is a fair proportion for fifty pounds in the sheaf to yield fifteen pounds of flax combed out. When spun into thread, it is rendered additionally supple by being soaked in water and then beaten out upon a stone; and after it is woven into a tissue, it is again beaten with heavy maces: indeed, the more roughly it is treated the better it is.

> Pliny, *Natural History*, 19.3

Julius Caesar, in *Gallic War*, recorded that British warriors 'dye their bodies with woad, which produce a blue colour' (Caesar, *Gallic War*, 5.14). Considerable processing is required to extract the blue dye that is locked away within the woad plant. Woad also had medicinal properties and the Greek physician Hippocrates recommended the application of woad leaves in the treatment of ulcers. Like flax, gold-of-pleasure may have been cultivated for the oil within its seeds. Oil could also be extracted from hemp, for which there is some slight evidence of its cultivation; of course, hemp could also be used to manufacture twine and rope.

Crops need to be harvested and stored in order to be of any use. Throughout prehistory the hand sickle was used to cut through the wheat or barley stems. Initially made of flint, or of wood with attached flint blades, sickles were later manufactured from bronze and then from iron. The Roman writer and agriculturalist Columella stated that it took one man a day and a half to reap a plot of land 73 m × 37 m (around one third of a hectare). Barley and wheat offer two products in one, both of equal value; the heads (or 'ears') provided a source of flour while the stems were put to use as cattle feed, roofing material, bedding for people and animals, and as a raw material in basketry.

Although straw must have been a source of winter fodder, hay (cut and dried grass) provides far more nutrients for animals. Hay was important as a winter food for any farmer with cattle, but it had to be kept dry or else it would rot and become useless. The single upright post-holes found at many settlement sites may represent an upright post around which a haystack (or a straw stack) could be built. A circular 'raft' of timbers was most likely laid at the base of the post to prevent the straw coming into contact the ground. Once straw has been stacked around this central post, it made sense to construct a tall thatched roof on top of the stack that would keep off the rain. Haystacks at the Butser Ancient Farm are constructed in this manner. In 2010 I spotted similar haystacks in southern Nepal, adjacent to the wattle and daub houses of the Chitwan farmers. These haystacks were also built around a single post, but unlike their British prehistoric cousins, they protruded from a wooden platform that rested on short stilts. Monsoon rains required the elevation of hay well away from the ground.

Some archaeologists believe that prehistoric farmers harvested just the ears of wheat and barley, returning later (or followed on behind by family members) to cut the stalks. Diodorus Siculus remarked of the Britons:

> The method they employ of harvesting their grain crops is to cut off no more than the heads and store them away in roofed granges, and then each day they pick out the ripened heads and grind them, getting in this way their food.

> Diodorus Siculus 5.21

Spelt almost requires this type of procedure, since this variety of wheat had to be parched before it could be threshed. Threshing is the beating or trampling of the sheaves of wheat to separate the grains from the inedible seed case (chaff) that surrounds it. Traditionally it takes place on a central threshing floor and is quickly followed by winnowing. Winnowing separates the now loose grains from the chaff that it is mixed up with, and in many societies this is done by tossing both into the air and catching only the grain while the breeze takes away the chaff. Imprints of chaff on some prehistoric pottery suggests that winnowing was done close to the roundhouse where activities like pottery making were going on.

Parching formed the final step in the processing of the cereal crop. We know that grain was baked before it went into storage. One storage pit at Itford Hill, Sussex, contained a large amount of parched barley grain while charred barley was found next to a grindstone inside a house on the Ness of Grunting, Shetland. A corn-drying oven found at Gwithian, Cornwall, dates from 1000 BC and illustrates the method by which farmers parched their grain. Parching was carried out to dry the grain in an attempt to lengthen its shelf life. Grain was stored as a food source that had to last a full year. The all-important cereal grains also had to be stored in a dry environment, and ideally one that was proof against rodents. During the Neolithic, grain was probably stored in sacks or pottery jars inside the house. Later, purpose-built wooden granaries were built that sat on four, six, or eight posts well away from hungry rodents and the damp ground. Their elevated position allowed air to circulate beneath the stored grain, an idea later used by the Romans in the construction of their own stone-built granaries, which all featured raised floors.

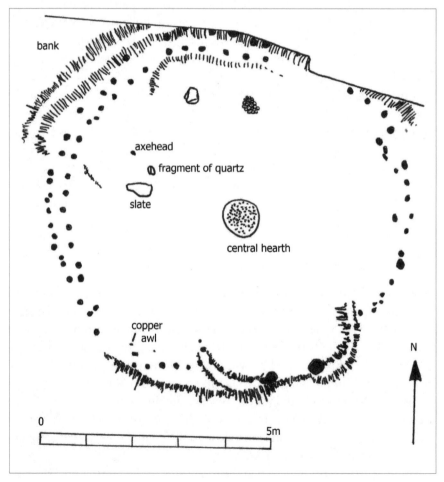

Roundhouse at Gwithian, Cornwall, which dates to the Early Bronze Age. (*K. Morton*)

Raised granaries were used during the Iron Age alongside the grain pit, an innovation that allowed farmers to safely deposit huge amounts of grain into cylindrical or bell-shaped pits cut into the bedrock. Capped with clay, these grain pits could be both watertight and proof against rodents. Diodorus Siculus commented that the ancient Britons 'dwell in mean cottages covered for the most part with reeds or sticks. In the reaping of their corn, they cut off the ears from the stalks and so house them in repositories underground' (Diodorus 5.16). Many of the storage pits that have been excavated have fairly large capacities and are deep enough to have held at least 1 ton of grain. An air tight seal kept moisture out and carbon dioxide (which was produced naturally by the stored grain) in—this inhibited any germination of the grains as well as the development of bacteria. Since a pit, once opened, could not be easily sealed again, it seems probable that most of them held, not cereals to be eaten, but seed corn in storage ready for planting next year. A single family would not be well-served by a high-capacity grain pit and a raised post granary would be much more accessible. Grain for consumption could be transferred in small amounts to the roundhouse and kept in jars or sacks ready for use. However, some pits were certainly holding grain in store for future meals: parched barley found in pits at both Itford and Fifield Bavant would never have sprouted, and clearly formed a large cache of food.

Livestock Farming

The prehistoric farm was mixed, rather than purely arable or pastoral. As we have seen, crop production and the raising of cattle was inextricably linked. Cattle and pigs were the first animals other than dogs to be domesticated in Britain and as the forest began to give way to more open, cleared countryside—sheep and goats were also introduced.

Throughout prehistory the breed of cattle dominating pastoral farming was the Celtic shorthorn, which closely resembled the modern Dexter cow. Cattle were resource rich, they provided milk and meat for human consumption as well as leather for the creation of bags, sacks, shoes, and items of clothing. In addition, their horns could be turned into an array of useful domestic items including cups, spoons, and combs. Dung dropped by cattle (amounting to around 25 kg per day) would have been collected and used to fertilise the fields. Archaeology suggests that cattle were kept together close to the roundhouse throughout the winter within corrals or round cattle sheds (byres). In Britain, this over-wintering period lasts almost 120 days, during which time the livestock must be close to a supply of winter fodder. Access to water, of which cattle need a good supply (something like 40 litres per day, per animal), must have been secured; although how this was managed is still not known.

Finally, the Celtic shorthorn brought muscle to the farm and served the prehistoric farmer as a tractor. Rock carvings, such as those at Val Camonic and Litsleby, show pairs of cattle working as a team and pulling ards across fields. They would also be useful in hauling carts and wagons, too—a wheel made of alder wood was unearthed at Flag Fen, dated to around 1300 BC. Throughout history, these pairs of trained animals were treated well and kept close to the farm, rather than be allowed to graze freely with the rest of the herd. Castration renders the bulls more docile and easier to control, and cattle given this treatment are known thereafter as oxen. Cattle were primarily kept as a source of meat and milk, but Iron Age Britons may also have bled their cattle during the winter and used the blood to mix with herbs and flour in order to make some form of black pudding. This was a renewable resource. In addition, many cattle bones from the prehistoric period show signs that they had been cracked and split to gain access to the edible marrow within.

During the Bronze Age it had been mainly the fabulous new metal bronze that marked one out as having wealth and power. The collection, hoarding, and giving of bronze items as gifts marked out the rich from the poor. As bronze trade networks fell away with the more local use of iron, bronze as a token of social currency also fell by the wayside. In the Iron Age, cattle now became the ultimate mark of a wealthy family, and it was not simply just the ownership of cattle that mattered, but the slaughter and consumption of the animals for food. This was feasting, conspicuous consumption, where the killing and eating of cattle and pigs was a social display, intended to impress. We are reminded of a similar practice from the Early Bronze Age burial mound at Irthlingborough, where scores of cattle were eaten and then buried with the deceased. Later Irish society was based around the concept of the *séd*, or milking cow, the value of which could be compared to other items. Two or three *séd* were equal to a *cumal*, the value of a female slave, and a measure of land (or varying quality and extent). A wonderful testament to the Iron Age emphasis on cattle is the 65,000-cubic-metre feasting midden (rubbish mound) at East Chisenbury, Wiltshire, dated to between 800 and 600 BC.

Production of both milk and beef involved a high degree of planning. Cows only produce milk after they have given birth to a calf, and then for only about ten months. Calves reach maturity in five or six years, after which they themselves can begin calving and producing milk. The danger for the farmer was that in letting cows have a calf every year in order to sustain the supply of milk, his herd would become so big that he could not provide enough fodder for it during the winter. A typical head of cattle chews through 15 kg of winter hay in a day. How many calves needed to be culled in order to maintain the herd? The farmer had to manage calving, milk production, and the butchery and storage of beef in a manner that could be sustained year after year.

Like cattle, sheep and goats were sources of meat, milk, and leather. Sheep, of course, were also an invaluable source of wool with which farm wives and their daughters made the family's clothes. In fact, judging by the 2:1 ratio of rams to ewes at many Iron Age sites both here and on the continent, it seems as if wool was far more important a resource than mutton or sheep's milk. The quality of wool taken from a large ram is generally superior to that of a smaller female.

Ancient sheep closely resembled the modern Mouflon or the Soay sheep breeds, being hardy and tough with brown coats. The fleece of Soay sheep do not need to be sheared, but are instead 'plucked' during the annual spring moult. In the Neolithic and Early Bronze Age, flocks could have been grazed on open land away from the farm's crops. With a greater degree of agricultural intensification during the Late Bronze and Iron Age, these animals are more likely to have been rotated around a number of fields closer to the roundhouse that were dedicated to pasture. Once they had manured the field and eaten the best of the grass they were probably moved on, and the field was then turned over to the growth of cereals or legumes. Winter fodder must also have been required for these animals, though of a lesser quantity, head-for-head, than cattle.

Both cattle and sheep had to be moved around the farming landscape and evidence from cropmarks and excavations have shown us how this was achieved. Field systems laid out from the Middle Bronze Age onwards show paddocks, farmyards, and fields linked together by tracks and purpose-built droveways. Dogs were undoubtedly used in handling both cattle and sheep and the bones of 'man's best friend' occur at many sites across Britain. Fields with corner gateways were excavated at Flag Fen, as well as a number of other sites, and these are ideally suited to funnelling animals to one particular point.

According to both historical references and the archaeological record, pork was popular feasting fare, indeed the pig had few uses other than meat and lard (used in cooking and the lighting of lamps). The Roman writer Strabo noted that the Celtic Gauls enjoyed 'large meals with milk and meat of all kinds, but most of all they loved pork, both fresh and salted. Their pigs run wild outdoors and are exceptional for their size, speed and strength' (Strabo 4.3). Pigs themselves did not require intensive livestock management and the most practical method would have been to let the pigs forage in nearby woodland. This kept the animals away from crops and had the effect of clearing away the woodland undergrowth. With voracious appetites and indiscriminate tastes, pigs could be let loose on arable fields after the harvest in order to dig out roots, remove weeds, and break up the soil. Most pigs were culled at a young age and only a small breeding stock, made up chiefly of females, would then be kept into adulthood. Modern attempts have been made to recreate the type of pig seen in Celtic figurines. This has been done by crossing wild boar with the oldest known British domesticated breed—the Tamworth. The resulting breed is known as an 'Iron Age' pig.

Little hard evidence exists for the domestication of geese, hens, and ducks, although the Celts as a whole were very fond of cooked goose. Pliny described roast goose as the most sumptuous dish known to the Britons. But did they hunt their geese and duck, or farm it? Chickens are recorded as food items on a grocery list found at Vindolanda Roman fort, close to Hadrian's Wall, and it is thought that the native Britons may also have kept and cooked these animals.

Woodland Management

From the very beginnings of agriculture in the British Isles, humans had managed the woodland landscape around them. Initially, forest had to be cleared to make way for pasture and arable land, but wood was an important resource and land clearance could not go unchecked. Pigs, for example, are at home in deciduous woodland and prefer to graze there; in particular, they prefer the marshy regions along forested valley floors. Other animals, too, were able to benefit from nearby woodlands. Peter Reynolds, the first director of Butser Ancient Farm, suggested that the traditional practice of collecting summer leaves for use as fodder in the winter was carried out in prehistoric times. Leaves would have been collected on their twigs and small branches, and fed to the goats and sheep. Peter noted that the Soay sheep at Butser preferred to browse on dried leaves if given the choice of either leaves or grass. To dry the woodland fodder, Peter's team erected simple drying racks upon which the leafy branches were hung. Adding weight to this theory, I often spotted goats sat around the front doors of farmhouses in southern Nepal, where the owners had strung up a handful of leafy twigs for them to graze on.

Of course, the greatest benefit that woodland can provide is a source of both fuel and building material. All roundhouses required a set of timber uprights and analysis has shown that there was a preference for oak posts—straight and of a diameter close to 30 cm. Trees of this size are typically between forty and sixty years old, which suggests that they were planted and carefully protected as a building material for the next generation. When it was realised that a roundhouse needed to be built, it was no good wandering through the woods looking for suitable trees. As in all things, the prehistoric farmer planned ahead. Wood was needed for the creation of tool handles, buckets, ards, fence posts, beds, doors, benches, carts, cartwheels, drinking troughs, and sundry other items.

Most fencing seems to have been of the wattle-hurdle type, where flexible hazel or willow rods were woven between a long series of upright timber posts. These fences were used to surround some arable fields (while others were bounded by raised banks, ditches, or hedges). Huge amounts of hazel would have been needed and its collection, like that of oak posts, could not be left to chance. Certainly Celtic farmers coppiced, that is cut shrubs or trees down to their stumps or roots in order to promote fresh growth. Numerous new stems emerge, growing straight up, and after several years the coppiced hazel tree provides perfectly suitable building material—long, straight hazel rods. In order to have a ready source of hazel rods throughout the year, the traditional technique of harvesting several coppiced areas (or 'coups') on a rotating basis, was probably practiced. Butser Farm experiments were able to demonstrate that a relatively modest 2.5 hectare site was able to provide over 500 tons of hazel rods for hurdle fencing.

Where hazel was not available, willow would have served the same purpose, although it was not as strong and lasted only half as long. Willow trees, of course, do not produce nuts. Charred hazelnut shells are found on many sites across the British Isles, which, together with the evidence for vast amounts of hazel rod fencing, suggest that hazel coppicing was a common feature of prehistoric farming. The competing requirements of hazel woodland needed careful management, however; coppiced hazel is best grown in shady areas within the forest, to encourage the shoots to grow straight upwards as they search for light. Hazelnuts, though, require sun and thrive on the edge of woodland. The need for two different resources from the same type of tree must have forced the farmer to dedicate certain coppiced hazels to one resource or another.

The role of firewood within a prehistoric community cannot be emphasized enough. As we shall see in Chapter 6, the central hearth served as the heart of every roundhouse. Fire flickered within the hearth throughout the day and to feed it an ever-replenishing stack of dry firewood had to be in place. Collection of firewood has been a daily task for women and children for millennia. As the sun set behind the slopes of Ngorongoro Crater, Tanzania, I watched Masaai children and women, in ones and twos, hurrying back to their homes laden with the firewood they had collected. Local woodland likewise served as the source of this unending prehistoric hunger for fuel.

As the metal age began, the hunger accelerated. The temperatures required to smelt copper or work iron were far higher than was needed to cook a stew. Only the heat provided by burning charcoal would do and an ever growing volume of it was needed. Charcoal is created by the slow 'roasting' of selected logs (alder is preferred) over a long duration either in a sealed pit, or in a charcoal pile. The pile technique leaves virtually no archaeological trace, but must have been used extensively in prehistory. A number of charcoal pits have been found, however, and a good example from the Iron Age was discovered at Laigh Newton, near Darvel in Scotland. Found a few metres from a temporary shelter, the excavators uncovered a rectangular pit 1.7 m × 1.1 m that was filled with a stack of charred timbers to a depth of 0.4 m. The base of the pit showed evidence of firing and a number of rounded stones in the pit suggested that the pit might even have been lined.

4

THE CELTIC YEAR

[The Fianna] divided the year into two parts. During the first half, namely from Beltane to Samhain, they hunted each day with their dogs; and during the second half, namely from Samhain to Beltane, they lived in their mansions...

The Pursuit of Giolla Dacker and his Horse,
a 16th century Irish tale

While we see time as an endless progression, with continual growth and improvement both desired and encouraged, the Celtic worldview was cyclical. Life was repeated endlessly, not just from year to year, but from generation to generation; this was a farming mind-set. According to the Roman writer Pliny, the Celtic year began and ended at its high point—Midsummer. Each day was reckoned to last from one sunset to the next, rather than from midnight to midnight as we do today.

Since the priests of the Celtic world—the druids—did not write anything down, we have only a vague idea of how the Celtic peoples measured time and how they celebrated their major festivals. In 1897, however, fragments of a bronze tablet were discovered at Coligny, in eastern France. Although the writing on the bronze sheet is in Latin script, the language is Gaulish, and, after a great deal of study, the archaeologist J. Monard came to the startling conclusion that the inscription represents a Celtic calendar.

The Coligny Calendar gives us a tantalizing glimpse into the Celtic world view. There were twelve months in most years, each month being containing twenty-nine or thirty days, making a Celtic year 354 days in length. Every month began at the full moon rather than the new moon, perhaps due to the fact that the full moon is easier to observe and record. An extra month, named Mid Samonios, was added every few years for intercalation, ensuring that the calendar kept pace with the seasons. Mid Samonios was slotted between the months called Cutios and Giamonios.

The Celtic Months

Month	Period	Length
Samonios	June–July	Thirty days
Dumannios	July–August	Twenty-nine days
Riuros	August–Sept	Thirty days
Anagantios	Sept–Oct	Twenty-nine days
Ogronios	Oct–Nov	Thirty days
Cutios	Nov–Dec	Thirty days
Giamonios	Dec–Jan	Twenty-nine days
Simivisionios	Jan–Feb	Thirty days
Equos	Feb–March	Twenty-nine days
Elembiuos	March–April	Twenty-nine days
Edrinios	April–May	Thirty days
Cantlos	May–June	Thirty days

If Pliny is correct, and the Celtic New Year began at Midsummer, then the first month was Samonios, during which the festival of Lughnasa was held. Both Lughnasa, as well as Beltane, which was an end of year celebration, were indicated on the Coligny calendar by small sigils. Two other major festivals, Imbolc and Samhain, are not indicated on the tablet. The etymology of the Celtic months is unclear, although some are more obvious than others. Samonios is most likely 'summer' and Giamonios is 'winter'; Riuros may be 'fat-time' (probably a reference to the harvest), Equos is almost certainly 'horsetime', and Cantlos is 'songtime'. Ogronios may perhaps refer to 'cold'.

Summer

> Bees with their little strength carry a load reaped from the flowers; the cattle go up muddy to the mountains; the ant has a good full feast.
>
> The corncrake is speaking, a loud-voiced poet; the high lonely waterfall is singing a welcome to the warm pool, the talking of the rushes has begun.
>
> The light swallows are darting ... the speckled salmon is leaping; as strong is the leaping of the swift fighting man.

The Boyhood Deeds of Finn mac Cumhaill, Laud 610

A year began at Midsummer and the farmer's first task would have been the making of hay. This fodder was going to keep the community's animals fed throughout the winter and the amount of fodder must have been directly related to the number of animals that had to be kept alive. Dry grass could have been cut from fallow fields (i.e. those fields left without a crop for that particular year) or alternatively areas of pasture might have been reserved for this purpose from spring until late summer. Ash and elm leaves were also probably gathered at this time for drying and they would go to supplement the hay.

Haymaking coincided with sheep shearing, since the native breeds shed their fleeces naturally in June. This meant that sheep could be 'plucked' rather than shorn. Farmers had to time this activity carefully, left too long and the sheep would rub off their moulting fleeces, but done too early and the fleece would not yet have fully developed. Bronze shears found at Flag Fen were initially thought to have been used for shearing, but experimental work with the Soay sheep now suggests that the shears were probably used for cutting cloth.

Bulls had to be mated with cows around this time of year to ensure that calves could be born in springtime, giving them the best chance of survival. This practice suggests that bulls were grazed apart from the herd for much of the year. However, it was the harvest that dominated late summer work and the culmination of a year's worth of effort by the family. There were two stages to a prehistoric harvest; those crops sown last autumn needed to be harvested first, followed by the crops that had been sown in spring. Harvesting was done with a great sense of urgency, a window of good weather was needed and if the farmer hesitated his entire crop might be spoilt. Crops were collected, processed, and stored in the shortest possible time, with everything edible put away for human use and the rest earmarked for animal feed. Unlike the stalks of modern wheat strains, cattle found emmer and spelt straw perfectly edible. During most of the Bronze Age as well as the Iron Age, dried crops and cereal grains were stored either in purpose-built granaries or in grain pits. Before that, crops were probably crammed inside the farmhouse.

Once cereal crops had been harvested, it was the turn of peas and beans. Some of these legumes would be put aside and eaten as green vegetables, but most would be dried and stored for consumption later in the year. Fruits, nuts, and berries were also likely to have been gathered at this time from well-known and regularly visited stands of trees and bushes. Other products that needed to be gathered including nettle stems (pounded and dried and woven together as thread), reeds (for thatching and basketry), and flax (with oil extracted from the seeds and fibres dried and combed to be turned into linen thread).

Midsummer was a high point for Celtic communities, a time of good weather, long days, healthy animals, and feasting and drinking. This period of comfort and plenty was associated with all the best that the Celtic afterlife had to offer. While Vikings, who were killed in battle, went either to Valhalla or Fólkvangr for a life of eternal combat, the Celtic paradise was Tir na Nog, a happy and abundant land of youth, a vast apple orchard where trees were forever in fruit. This says much about the Celtic outlook on life and death, on what was valued and appreciated. The Viking looked forward to endless bloodshed, while the Celt anticipated a paradise of fruit trees and agricultural abundance.

Lughnasa was the first big festival of the Celtic year and may have lasted a whole month. Today it is allocated to 1 August, but prehistoric communities almost certainly marked their festivals by the counting of full moon lunations. Lughnasa in one particular year, for example, might have been held in the third or fourth full moon after Midsummer. Members of the Iron Age priesthood, the Druids, will have kept a more careful account and disseminated the fact that the lunation had changed and that the festival was going to be a full moon earlier, or later, than it had been the year before. Lugh was an oak god known throughout Celtic Europe, he was a folk hero and several Roman towns bore his name. Lughnasa fell between the hay harvest and the wheat harvest and was probably a commemoration of Lugh's death. Funerary rites and processions must have taken place, using effigies or even living substitutes. Lugh was a barley-god, a sun-hero, who had to die so that the community might live another year. Rites that re-enacted the death of Adonis, Tammuz, and John Barleycorn have featured in traditional European folklore for over two millennia. He is cut by the reapers' sickles, trampled on the threshing floor, and finally crushed beneath the millstone. A local Lincolnshire rite involved burying a straw effigy of John Barleycorn in the fields once the harvest had been completed:

> *They ploughed, they sowed, they harrowed him in,*
> *Throwed clods upon his head.*
> *And these three men made a solemn vow:*
> *John Barleycorn was dead.*

'John Barleycorn', traditional song

The ancestry of the straw doll, fashioned each year only to be destroyed, represents the harvest god and his ultimate demise at the hands of men. Names of the gods vary from place to place and from age to age, but the tradition persisted throughout European history. Ancestor spirits may also have been remembered at Lughnasa, marriages may also have been more frequent and the stations of kings and chiefs were likely to have been confirmed.

Autumn

The ox is lowing, the winter is creeping in, the summer is gone. High and cold the wind, low the sun, cries are about us; the sea is quarrelling.

The Boyhood Deeds of Finn mac Cumhaill, Laud 610

Following the rush to harvest in late summer, crucial follow-up work was necessary. It was vital that the ground was prepared for a new crop. Work done here would have important repercussions for the family's survival in a year's time. After the fields were sufficiently manured, ploughing with the ard could begin. Planting then followed, typically using seed gathered the year before that had been held in reserve for that purpose. By far the best candidates for an autumn sowing were emmer, spelt, and barley.

Why were crops sown before winter, when the cold temperatures and regular frosts would not give the seed chance to grow? Was it not better to wait until the early spring? It was a case of spreading the workload. The autumn crop would mature earlier in the summer than one sown in spring, resulting in a staggered harvest. This allowed a community to maximise its limited manpower and the amount of cultivated land that it could successfully manage. Also, the frosts of early spring could have a pruning effect on new shoots similar to the way in which farmers coppiced hazel trees by aggressively cutting them back. When frost occurs (where snow does not lay on the ground, to blanket and insulate the seed) it can kill young shoots, forcing a profusion of new ones to emerge from the plant's root. These energetic new shoots are called tillers, and they lead to more abundant harvests. Of course, frost still posed a great danger to the young and vulnerable crops. A long, frost-filled winter with little snow could kill the crops dead in the fields, leaving the community with nothing to harvest in the summer. Frost-prone areas included valley bottoms and higher ground.

The fields that were about to be sown with an autumn crop were treated with manure first. Sheep or cattle grazed on the fields so that they could drop manure directly where it was needed, while simultaneously rooting through the soil to dig out weeds. Ploughing had to follow quickly, lest concentrations of animal manure burned the ground (potentially leaving an infertile 'scar' on the field for some years to come). Weeds missed by the animals were then hoed out by hand before the soil was ploughed and furrows would then have been levelled—perhaps by dragging a log behind an ox. Once the ground had been prepared, a seed-drill ard was used to cut a fine furrow and seed would then have been planted within it.

Families faced long, dark days ahead and any animals that could not be fed with the fodder in hand had to be killed. Sheep, cattle, and pigs not needed for breeding would be slaughtered first, although an efficient farmer would have planned to store an adequate amount of fodder and limit the number of animals that he had to cull. Older ewes and young rams would be likely candidates. Processing a butchered animal would have been labour intensive, particularly since the meat required drying, smoking, or salting; it was then stored up in the rafters of the roundhouse. For the rest of the herd, the last days of autumn were spent grazing on the fields, eating up the last of the grass in order to preserve as much winter fodder as possible.

After the autumnal equinox, the next great festival was Samhain, which today is allocated to 1 November. Modern Halloween is now closely associated with this traditional Celtic festival, although it actually owes far more to the Christian festival of All Hallows Eve. Samhain marked the end of summer and the beginning of winter, a point that divides the warmer half of the year from the colder. It was a festival during which livestock were rounded up and decisions made about which were to be overwintered and which would be killed. It was also a time when spirits were propitiated with offerings of food and drink and where the souls of the dead revisited their homes.

Winter

The ferns are reddened and their shape is hidden; the cry of the wild goose is heard; the cold has caught the wings of the birds; it is the time of ice-frost, hard, unhappy.

The Boyhood Deeds of Finn mac Cumhaill, Laud 610

One might think that the prehistoric peasant spent his winter indoors, huddled around the fire while icy blasts of wind rattled the timbers of his house. Unfortunately, this luxury was not open to him, there were jobs to be done that he and his family simply did not have time for in the spring, summer, or autumn.

Fallow fields, or new land that was earmarked for cultivation, had to be ploughed in order that frost action during the winter months might break down the soil. Away from the fields, a great deal of activity took place within local woodland. Trees were now bare of leaves and their sap had stopped rising. Now was the time to coppice stands of hazel and willow. A large amount of wood was needed for new fencing or for repairs. Other trees were exploited—the raw material for tool handles, hundreds of fence posts, and the timbers for any new buildings that were planned. Ash and oak would be the preferred tree for these tasks, with the offcuts going straight into the farm's wood store.

Daily tasks would have included general repairs around the farm, the roundhouse thatch would need regular maintenance and shelters, byres, and corrals might need constructing, repairing, or modifying. Animals required far more attention in winter than at other times of the year since they were now fed by hand from supplies of fodder, rather than left to graze freely on pasture land. Seed had to be prepared for sowing later in the year and this involved breaking it down from the reaped ear to the naked seed. This seed corn was put into storage for the coming year—without it, the community would have nothing to sow.

Alignments at Stonehenge, Newgrange, and other Neolithic and Bronze Age monuments reflect the importance of the Midwinter solstice festival. Astronomically, it marks the shortest day as well as the longest night of the year. Our modern calendar usually places the winter solstice on 21 December; for farmers in prehistoric Northern Europe this was the darkest of times, when the long days and bountiful harvests of summer must have seemed so far away.

Traditional festivals that involve the Yule Candle or Yule Log are almost certainly derived from a Celtic origin. Although 'yule' is a Middle English term, early Welsh texts (particularly the Romance of Amergin) certainly describe the Yule Log's association with fire and its symbolic links with the sun god. Selecting, cutting, and transporting the Yule Log indoors was always done with great ceremony. The blessing of the sun god was brought indoors with the log itself, which stood as a symbol of light in the darkness of winter. Traditionally, many superstitions were associated with the Yule Log: it could be neither bought nor sold, but it could be stolen, cut from one's own land, or accepted as a gift. It was often decorated with evergreen branches before being dragged to the house for burning, and, before it was lit, the log was sprinkled with grains of wheat or a favoured alcoholic drink. Bad luck would follow if the log failed to burn steadily or went out, and once midwinter was over, the remains of the log were stored and used to safely ignite next year's Yule Log. These superstitions reflect rituals that have their origins in the prehistoric past.

Now allocated to 1 February, the late winter festival of Imbolc marked the very beginning of spring. It was dedicated to the goddess Brigit, whose name was also taken up by the powerful northern tribe that called itself the Brigantes. Imbolc, like the goddess herself, was associated with childbirth and motherhood. This was a time of very obvious signs of growth and regeneration within the countryside. Shoots emerged from the ground and wild animals, such as badgers, began to stir from their slumber. Imbolc may also have been associated with the first lambing.

Spring

It is the month of May, a pleasant time; its face is beautiful; the blackbird sings his full song, the living wood is his holding, the cuckoos are singing and ever singing.

There is a welcome before the brightness of the summer.

The Boyhood Deeds of Finn mac Cumhaill, Laud 610

Spring was welcomed—frosts were fewer, the weather was warmer, and the working day was longer. The first flowers were a sign of the coming spring and some, like coltsfoot and primrose, were a source of salves and medicines. Spiky gorse bushes erupted in yellow flowers and catkins appeared on the willow tree. These were good signs, willow was a valuable material used in basketry and fencing. The thorny gorse bush, too, could be used to quickly erect a stock proof corral.

As the weather improved, the cattle could be led out of their byres. This gave the farmer an opportunity to clean out a winter's worth of manure, load it onto carts, and spread it onto the land. More ploughing followed in order to mix this manure into the soil. Lambing began in spring ready to take full advantage of the long grass that had recently grown up in the pastures. Calves were also born and led to fresh pastures along with their mothers. Male calves, not earmarked as breeding stock, would be fed by their mothers throughout the summer and by the start of winter they would be fattened and ready for slaughter. Farmers had to take care, though; livestock that had spent months overwintering were susceptible to disease in the still chilly and often damp pastures.

Each day of decent weather was exploited to the full and ploughing was soon followed by the sowing of the spring crop. Cereals like barley, oats, and spelt were sown first, followed by peas and Celtic beans. While cereals were a little hardier, legumes were more susceptible to frost, hence the need for a later sowing. Flax was most likely last in the sowing sequence, since its seedlings were extremely vulnerable to periods of frost.

Beltane, a great end-of-year festival, was held before the year began again in Midsummer. The god Bel or Belinus was worshipped across Celtic Europe, he was the 'Shining One', typically associated with fire and sunlight. Beli Mawr ('Great Beli') appears in The Mabinogion as the founder of the Welsh royal line and as the King of Britain. The primary ceremony, carried out at Beltane, involved driving the community's livestock between two fires in order to purify and heal them. This must have been a difficult task, no doubt dogs were used to help and the entire community will have participated. Following this Druidic ritual, the sheep and cattle were taken out to new pastures.

In late spring, the crops that now began to stand in the fields had to be frequently weeded with hoes, a vital job that ensured the crop was not swamped. The sowing of seed in narrow drills, or furrows, left dead space between them that could be weeded more effectively than a seed scatter might be. Experiments at Butser Ancient Farm have demonstrated that at least three good sessions of hoeing were needed to clean out weeds amongst a field of wheat or barley.

Since honey provided the only real sweetener available to the Celtic tribes (other than fruit), beekeeping was practised by many communities. Bees swarmed in late spring. The imminent emergence of a new queen, raised within the hive by the worker bees, forces the old queen out and she takes with her at least half of the hive. They set out to build a new hive at this time of the year. Honey was used not just as an additive in food, but also as an essential ingredient in the fermentation of mead—a popular Celtic drink.

5

TOOLS

Farming requires farm tools. This seems an obvious statement, but the tools required must fit the job and on any farm, whether arable or dairy (or mixed, as most prehistoric farms seem to have been), the jobs were many and varied. What tools should we expect a family engaged in mixed farming to possess? And what can be found in the archaeological record?

Plough

We have already discussed the development of the prehistoric plough (the ard) in Chapter 3. One or more ards would have been crucial to any mixed farming enterprise. Each ard would have been a valuable asset and its construction would have first required the careful selection of certain shapes of wood. Those parts of the ard that received the most wear and tear, particularly the share, were made of stone (and later iron).

Spade

Wooden spades fitted with metal 'shoes' that protect the cutting edge are commonly found in Roman museums across Europe. Unfortunately, finds of these useful tools are rarely represented in the prehistoric record. There are some wooden 'spade-like tools', but none can be definitively identified. However, spade marks have been found on several archaeological sites.

Hoes

Hoes are clearly depicted in one of the Val Camonic rock carvings from northern Italy. One man breaks up clods of earth behind the ard with his hoe, while another man carries his hoe ready as he leads the ox team across the field. Stone, antler, or flint heads are likely to have been mounted onto the ends of these hoes. A common type of flint tool from the Neolithic called a 'rod' or 'fabricator' is thought to have been the business end of a hoe. Each 'rod' is a heavy flint shape, long and narrow, with almost a square section. Mounted on a wooden handle at 90 degrees, these flint tools would have made excellent hand hoes.

Digging sticks are primitive hoes that are still an important tool in hunter-gatherer cultures today. Essentially a sharpened and fire-hardened length of wood, the digging stick is used for digging up roots, for turning over the soil, as a spade, and as a method of digging holes for the planting of seeds. Digging sticks must have been used in the Mesolithic and doubtless continued to be useful throughout the Neolithic period. A number of ancient antler points, sporting a hole that has been bored through one end, have been interpreted as the hoe-like heads for prehistoric digging sticks.

Sickles

Metal sickles were used to harvest crops and cut fodder for animals in both the Bronze and Iron Age. Prior to the metal ages, crops were either uprooted or cut using flint sickles. These earlier flint sickles were fashioned in one of two ways; the first, and most common, was the mounting of several small and irregularly shaped flint blades on to the inner edge of curved wooden handles (and such sickles are also known from ancient Egypt). During the Late Neolithic, expert flint knappers in southern Britain were able to go one step further and create beautiful one-piece sickle blades.

With the onset of the Bronze Age a number of sickle-shaped metal blades emerge and, rather than attempt to categorize these tools by the job they may have performed, it is simpler, and perhaps more pragmatic, to accept that they served as multi-purpose tools. Bronze, and later iron, was an expensive material that will have necessitated an adaptable approach to tool use. Knobbed (or 'button') sickles occur in the Middle Bronze Age, while the more sophisticated riveted and socketed types are found only from the Late Bronze Age onward.

The Iron Age led to a great variety of curved blades being used in agriculture, some of which may have been used primarily for harvesting, others for pruning and many (I am sure) for both. The emergence of the classic billhook shape appears during the British Iron Age, here the main part of the blade is straight like a heavy knife, with only the tip curved. Reaping hooks are more generally curved throughout their length. Some commentators have associated this new type of tool with a deteriorating Iron Age climate and the necessity to collect winter fodder. I believe, however, that the increased supply of iron allowed for more specialisation in blade shapes, and that, in previous ages, fodder would have been cut using the bronze sickle or its flint equivalent.

Pitchforks

Handling large amounts of straw and hay required the use of a rake or pitch fork. Presumably these were made of wood and so their remains are rarely discovered. Excavations on the Somerset Levels did reveal one ancient pitchfork, and although it was probably used to lift rushes rather than straw, it certainly illustrates that the prehistoric farmer had this tool in his inventory. I have used some beautifully made reconstructions, the most striking of which was a single piece of branch that had been carefully selected by its maker for the job. A single straight bough served as the fork's handle and at its end the fork split naturally into four smaller branches. These had been shaped with steam, then shortened and sharpened to form the 'forks' of the pitchfork.

The Neolithic axe quarry at Langdale Pikes in the Lake District is still littered with worked blades, fragments, and waste. Axes were produced from the fine greenstone of the mountain and then transported across Britain. While most of the stones here are blades with symmetrically worked edges, the piece on the far right is a large, 19-cm-long flake, produced during the axe-making process. (*Author's collection*)

Axes

Axes of stone or flint were used in the Neolithic period and they served as an important multi-purpose tool, powering the agricultural way of life. Certain types of stone were especially prized as material for axe production and the quarries were located at sites in the rugged western fringes of Britain. From there axes were 'exported' to communities further afield. By far the most important quarry (producing perhaps the best or the most prestigious stone axe-heads) was the site atop the Langdale Pikes, a group of stunning mountain peaks at the heart of the Lake District. The grand vistas and imposing pinnacle, known as the Pike o' Stickle at the mountain's summit, certainly impress a visitor today. Hiking to the top, I was amazed to find thousands of waste pieces littering the summit, most chipped from roughed-out axe-

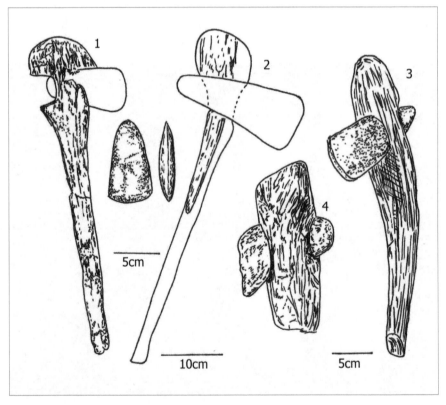

Rare wooden axe hafts from the Neolithic.
1. Shulishader, Isle of Lewis.
2. Etton, Cambridgeshire.
3. Edercloon, County Longford.
4. County Monaghan.
(*F. Pryor and A. Sheridan*)

heads. Langdale Pike is also remarkable for a wide grassy area close to the peak that surely must have served as the summer camping ground for the quarry workers and their families. Did western tribes make their livings from quarrying stone axe 'blanks' and trading them to others? Some axe finds from the Neolithic are finely polished, creating almost a work of art, a highly prized object that could be traded, given as a gift or used. Some found their way here from Ireland and a small number of exotic greenstone axes had been imported all the way from the Alps.

The axe had an obvious use in felling trees either for forest clearance or timber. Boats, looms, wagons, and lathes required good timber as did the pillars for roundhouses, ploughs, and fence posts. Countless other wooden items also depended on the existence of the axe: ladders, stools, benches, beds, animal traps, shelters, bows, spears, tool handles, frames for stretching skins, and others for drying or smoking meat. Axes (probably of different sizes) were used to fell the tree, remove its branches, split logs, and shape wood. Did every adult male possess his own axe, or perhaps more than one if he was of a high status? Over 20,000 stone axes of Irish origin have already been found, many more than anticipated.

With the onset of the Early Bronze Age, axes were cast first in copper and then in bronze. These first blades are known as 'flat axes' since they were simply the product of pouring molten metal into an open mould. A rapid technological progression soon followed, axes began to be cast with flanges in order that they might better grip their wooden haft, but soon palstave types and socketed types were produced. The remains of a Bronze Age timber circle, known as Seahenge, which was uncovered on a beach at Holme-next-the-Sea in Norfolk, was carefully studied by timber experts. The unique cut marks of between fifty and sixty individual bronze axes were identified on the Seahenge timbers. This probably illustrates the work of an entire community on one large project. Axes developed in the Iron Age differ little from those found in hardware stores today; there has been almost no improvement on that design in the past 2,000 years.

6

THE ROUNDHOUSE

When several [Celts] dine together, they sit in a circle; but the mightiest among them, distinguished above the others for skill in war, or family connexions, or wealth, sits in the middle...

Athenaeus 4.151

Visiting a reconstructed roundhouse is a special event; standing inside that circular domestic space you can imagine the repetitive sound of grain being ground on the millstone, the hissing and crackling of the fire, perhaps even the snores of family members, sleeping in the dark. I've been lucky enough to spend several weekends with friends living in a roundhouse at the Ryedale Folk Museum, North Yorkshire. Of a typical Iron Age size, the house sits between a wheat field and a small wetland area. A tree-lined field opposite the entrance has held Soay sheep and Iron Age pigs, at different times.

Cooking, working, and sleeping inside the house gave a flavour of what it must have been like to call a roundhouse home. Each experience provided an insight: cooking in poor light, sleeping in straw-lined beds while a mouse scurried past, grinding enough flour for the daily bread, and managing the fire to maximise light and flame while minimizing smoke.

Any discussion of prehistoric cookery has to address the importance of the Celtic roundhouse, for it was not just kitchen and dining hall, but also storeroom and farmhouse. From around 2000 BC roundhouses began to replace the earlier rectangular structures that had been built during the Neolithic. At the same time, circular Beaker barrows began to proliferate and it may have been their design that influenced the new shape of housing. Within 300 years, the arrangement of Bronze Age houses become almost standardized, with many examples from across the British Isles displaying similar floor plans, probably reflecting a shared belief system or way of life. British farmers felt an affinity with the roundhouse that lasted up until the arrival of the Saxons and Angles, a period of history that spans 2,400 years (equivalent to almost eighty human generations).

The Structures

Roundhouses varied in diameter, but a large number of excavated examples are somewhere between 5 and 7 metres. Typically, a low circular wall was made of wattle and daub and above it stood a conical roof of thatch or turf that was supported by a spoked arrangement of timbers. Small houses were able to rely on this spoked-wheel design of rafters to support the weight of the roof. For larger buildings, more substantial support was needed, typically in the form of a ring of sturdy posts within the floorplan of the roundhouse. With the weight now borne by both the outer wall and the inner ring of posts, this type of house is termed a double-ring structure. Triple-ring houses have also been discovered that had recourse to yet another ring of posts within the centre of the house, allowing for a greater diameter and a commensurate increase in living space.

Not all of the outer walls were built of wattle fences and strengthened with daub, some were constructed from banks of earth while others were formed from drystone; methods and materials varied from one region to another according to local tradition and available resources. One of the remarkable features of roundhouse architecture is the orientation of their single, timber-framed doorways. The vast majority of entrances face south-east or east, which correlates to the direction of the morning sun. A great deal has been written on the association of the roundhouse with a sun cult or a cosmological belief in a sun-orientated world view. Other archaeologists see the orientation of the doorway more as a practical matter. There were no smoke holes or chimneys in the roof and no windows in the walls; consequently, these buildings would have been dark and smoky places in which to live.

There are few isolated examples of excavated roundhouses, more commonly they are found in clusters of between two and ten, indicative of a small hamlet or a community of related families. While some of these communities were surrounded by earthen banks and ditches or by timber fences, there are plenty of examples that remained 'unenclosed'. The settlement at Mucking, which overlooked the Thames, dates from the Late Bronze Age and there, an impressive double-banked circular enclosure surrounded two roundhouses. Meanwhile at Blackpatch, Sussex, five roundhouses from the same period sat within an enclosure marked out by a stout fence. Dartmoor, rich in building stone, yielded a stone-walled enclosure at Shaugh Moor. Inside this 50-m-diameter settlement sat five stone-walled houses, some complete with cobbled yards. Not all of these structures served as dwellings, some are smaller than others and, at Shaugh Moor, pottery finds and the analysis of phosphate levels left behind by animal manure indicate that while the largest house was used for human habitation, the others were a mixture of outhouses and byres. Even then, phosphate research showed that the family home had been shared with farm animals from time to time.

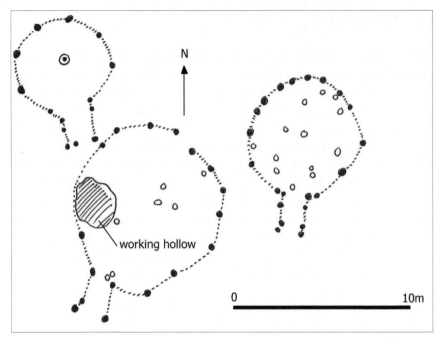

Bronze Age roundhouses at Winterbourne Stoke, Wiltshire. (*S. Garrett*)

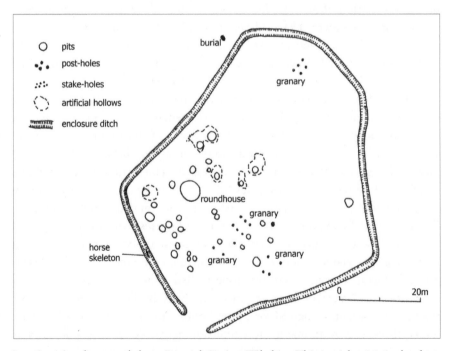

Late Iron Age farmstead, from Berwick Down, Wiltshire. This is a 'classic' single-phase farm with roundhouse, granaries, enclosure ditch, spacious farm yard, and working pits. (*G. J. Wainwright*)

Light and Dark

Without windows, the main source of light for the inhabitants of a roundhouse would have been the door. Some houses were constructed with a porch or roofed extension over the doorway that provided much needed shelter from wind and rain. A door of wood or leather would have been closed at night, but left open during the day. Post-built structures (those with at least one inner ring of supporting posts) may have had a gap between the thatched roof and the top of the outer wall, which would have allowed additional light to spill into the house in the early morning. This gap was hidden from unwanted bad weather by the overhanging eaves.

Obviously the best lit area of the house was directly in front of the doorway. However, the movement of the sun throughout the day meant that the illuminated areas of the house changed. Let us say that the doorway faced due south; the early morning sun shone from the south-east and would have lit up the area directly in front of the doorway as well as the north-western portion of the room. By mid-morning the area lit by the sun had shifted from left to right and now the shaft of sunlight illuminated both the centre of the room and backspace, opposite the doorway. Shadows lengthened in the afternoon, and the sun's light shifted over to the north-eastern side of the roundhouse. By late afternoon or evening, a fire would have been needed to provide any useful light. Throughout the day the darkest parts of the house were the left and right peripheries at the side of the room, as well the roof-space, above.

Discussion of light patterns within the roundhouse is not theoretical, but practical. There were many activities that had to be conducted indoors. Spinning and weaving were carried out, grain had to be ground and baked as bread. Cloth was sewn, clothes were mended or made, meat and vegetables had to be prepared and cooked over the fire, flint tools needed fabricating, animal hides were cleaned, treated and stretched, baskets were woven, and bone, antler, and horn was worked to create tools and other artefacts. Finally there was a need for socializing, resting, and sleeping.

If the weather permitted, it is likely that many activities were conducted outside the house, but wet or cold weather would quickly have driven these activities inside. Harsh winter weather will have forced the inhabitants to shut the door and so rely on light from the fire for their daily activities. Lamps of butter or animal fat might have been used to supply light, but this was a food resource 'going up in smoke'. More than likely, prehistoric farmers relied on flames from the fire for light during the evening.

Entranceways into roundhouses generally focussed on the east and south-east to maximise the amount of sunlight available. Additionally, with a prevailing wind in Britain that blows from the west-south-west, the east facing doorways provided a level of shelter. Differences in latitude can be traced in the ground plans of many roundhouses, with more northerly houses in the Highlands of Scotland facing south-east, those in southern Scotland and northern England facing mainly east-south-east and roundhouses further south orientated more towards the east. The further north the communities lived, the fewer daylight hours were available to them in winter. Doorway orientations were tailored to maximise the provision of winter daylight.

The Hearth

No one would deny that the hearth formed the centre of life in a prehistoric roundhouse, and it is therefore fitting that in most houses it is precisely where the hearth can be found—at its centre. Some examples are found elsewhere, but the overwhelming majority are located at the centre point, or (less commonly) slightly forward, towards the door. In practical terms this is the most obvious location, since it provides an even distribution of light and heat. In addition, the risk of an accidental fire is reduced, since a fire near to the periphery might easily spread to the wattle wall, or the thatched roof, which is at its lowest as it passes over the outer wall. Conversely, the highest point of the roof, its apex, sits exactly over the centre of the roundhouse and sparks travelling upwards lose their heat well before they reach the vulnerable thatch.

Visitors to the house at Ryedale Folk Museum often comment on the lack of a chimney or smoke hole. This design feature is based on several decades' worth of experimental building. Some of the first replica roundhouses that were constructed in the 1950s included such a feature. However, in the same way that a fierce draught can be created in a small house by opening both the front and back doors simultaneously, the smoke hole drew up the hot air from the fire and the sparks with it. More than one of these experimental houses was burned down after the thatch caught fire. Instead, the smoke and hot air rises into the conical roof space, with smoke seeping slowly out of the thatch. Sparks that are carried up enter this oxygen-less zone and are extinguished with virtually no risk to the roof. On waking up within the roundhouse in the early hours of the morning, I noticed that the air was very smoky and that clothing and bedding smelt strongly of smoke. All the occupants were coughing, despite having little problem with smoke the day before. I suspect that the dying fire and the lack of any upward air current allowed the smoke that had built up within the roof space to fall back into the living area. Was the thatch too thick? Should it have been thinner in order to let the smoke out more rapidly?

Hearths are usually nothing more than circular or rectangular areas marked out by high-sided stone slabs. These retained the ashes and prevented burning logs from rolling across the roundhouse floor. It is not a camp fire;

the prehistoric hearth was a major area of domestic activity and had to be big enough to support several cook pots at once. Likewise, it had to be big enough to allow three or four people to stir food, move pots, and tend the fire. When my colleagues and I put on a cooking demonstration for the public, one of us kept the fire going, while another made bean cakes and was frying them on a flat stone in one corner of the hearth. Meanwhile another cook baked eggs in the ashes and yet another tended the spit, upon which a duck was being slowly roasted. We discovered that different types of fire were required simultaneously, with hot ashes being enough to bake the eggs, but flames needed to roast the duck. Our bean cake fryer needed only very moderate heat to bring his flat cooking stone to the temperature that he needed. In this way the hearth served many purposes at once, a little like the Victorian kitchen range that used a single coal fire to heat a water boiler, an oven, and one or more stoves.

Baskets of dry wood and/or charcoal would have been kept adjacent to the hearth perhaps along with a number of benches. These benches might be fixed or moveable, but experience has shown that they are not placed too close to the fire. Access is always needed to manage the fire as well as whatever might be cooking on it, and so a decent 'kneeling space' is best left around the edge of the hearth.

Internal Arrangement

Rarely do roundhouses survive in the ground as anything more than infilled post-holes and stained areas of soil. It is difficult, then, to determine whether a roundhouse may or may not have had a second floor, used perhaps for sleeping and for storage. This is an idea first developed by Diana Reynolds in 1982. Double-ring structures do have the structural integrity to support a second floor and approximately 20–30 per cent of their total volume lies above the ring beam up inside the roof, which essentially becomes 'dead space'. Were full, or partial, attics used? Double and triple ring structures were certainly strong enough to bear the weight, but it is interesting to note that although smaller (7–9 metre diameter) single-ring houses were quite able to support a roof without any internal posts, some were found with a second inner ring of posts. This was overbuilding, and whether it took place for structural security, status, or the support of an upper floor, we cannot know. Wooden steps or ladders would have allowed access to this upper floor.

Finds recovered from prehistoric roundhouses indicate that different activities took place in different areas of the house. The well-lit space around the hearth and in front of the doorway seems to have been the focus of craft activities and food preparation. Leather and bone-working, sewing and weaving all require decent light levels. Talking, sleeping, resting, and storage need very little light and were therefore relegated to the periphery of the roundhouse, to the outer edges and the backspace, behind the hearth. It was here that some measure of privacy could be had. This front-versus-back division is often observed amongst the modern roundhouse dwellers of today, people like the Galla and Dorze from Ethiopia, as well as the Kipsigis from Kenya.

Pits were a common feature of roundhouses and were used, it seems, mainly for storage. These pits were commonly dug at the front of the house, or else at the back of the structure. In a house from South Shields, pits and grain processing debris were found between the hearth and the doorway, while bedding material was found at the back. Meanwhile, a house at Tormore on the Isle of Arran contained a pair of post holes near the doorway, indicative of a vertical weaving loom and there was evidence of flint knapping and both crop and wood processing in the area. Tormore revealed that grain and timber had been stored towards the back of the roundhouse.

Roundhouse using cultures today place their furniture around the periphery of the house, leaving the central area fairly clear. Studies have shown that this cluttered periphery is typically around 1.7 metres in width and covers more area than the central space. In one of these 10-metre-diameter houses, the periphery accounted for around 62 per cent of the total floor space, with the central area making up the remaining 38 per cent. We can assume similar patterns of use in British prehistory, where the central area around the hearth and the well-lit front space were important for work, while the periphery was utilised mainly for living and storage. At Greaves Ash, Northumberland, a roundhouse was discovered that featured a paved periphery, clearly marking out the importance of this space to the inhabitants. At the Ryedale Folk Museum, two double beds have been constructed in the Iron Age roundhouse at the eleven o'clock and one o'clock positions (as one enters the house at the six o'clock position). Both wooden beds are straw-filled wooden boxes, able to hold two or three sleepers with ease and covered by a platform supported on four posts. This platform serves as a place for the storage of baskets.

The circular periphery, running around the inside of the roundhouse wall, would have held beds, straw-filled mattresses ('paillasses'), firewood, equipment and tools, food, shields and weaponry, and also animals. Although circular stables and byres are a common feature of Celtic farms, there is evidence that some roundhouses were inhabited by both humans and cattle. In southern Scotland and parts of England phosphate analysis has shown that cattle were very likely to have been kept inside many of the region's roundhouses over winter. Studies of phosphate levels within the peripheral areas of roundhouses at Dalnaglar in Perthshire, Shaugh Moor in Dartmoor, Morl y Gerddi in Gwynedd, and Lintchie Gutter in Lanarkshire indicated the stalling of animals there. Families may have slept within other parts of the periphery or, alternatively, on a second floor. This may not represent the entire herd, rather it would have been younger animals and their mothers, or animals that needed to be kept close for milking.

Around half of the modern roundhouse using cultures today stall their animals (mainly cows, calves, and goats) inside their houses. Larger roundhouses like the double and triple-ring structures, are more likely to be used in this way, i.e. bigger houses were more likely to accommodate some of the family's animals. Typically the animals are just stalled overnight and kept behind a partition, but one tribe, the Kenyan Kipsigis, let their sheep settle freely while the family sleeps on an upper floor. The practice of bringing animals into the house is common throughout Africa, just as it was in Medieval Britain. The advantages of doing this in winter are raised temperatures within the roundhouse and easy access to the animals for the collection of dung, or for the milking of cows and goats.

Being warm and dry, roundhouses were the perfect place for the storage of equipment, tools, firewood, and foodstuffs. People using roundhouses today store their belongings and food supplies in a variety of ways: in string bags hung from the rafters, on racks suspended from the roof, on a raised attic or upper floor, on shelves or pegs mounted on the outer wall, or on hooks driven into the inner posts. Warm air and smoke rising up into the roof space meant that prehistoric farmers could use this area to store food on a medium or long term basis. Smoke will have inhibited the growth of bacteria, prolonging the life of meat and cheese and the dry warm air will have kept crops (like grains, beans, and peas) dry and free from damp. Firewood was most likely dried out under the over-hanging eaves of the house (as the Kenyan Kikuyu do today), or beneath a purpose-built wood shelter. At regular intervals, perhaps even daily, firewood was transferred indoors so that it was thoroughly dry before burning.

In prehistory, as in many parts of modern Africa, the immediate area in front of the house became an extension of the interior. For the Tswana tribe, this area provides space to store building materials, for a vegetable or herb garden, for animal pens, for a toilet and a washing area, for the storage of animal feed, and as an outdoor kitchen. At prehistoric sites in Britain, the areas outside and between roundhouses are dominated by fence lines or ditches as well as post-built rectangular structures (these might represent wood stores, toilets, store sheds, and granaries). The fence lines suggest that the control of animals in the immediate environs of the house was crucial and that mixed farming was important, as we already suspect. Ditch or fence lines also separate hungry animals from crops, again suggesting that vegetables may have been cultivated right on the doorstep.

Rubbish tips, what archaeologists term 'middens', are not common finds close to roundhouses. It may be that waste was routinely deposited onto the

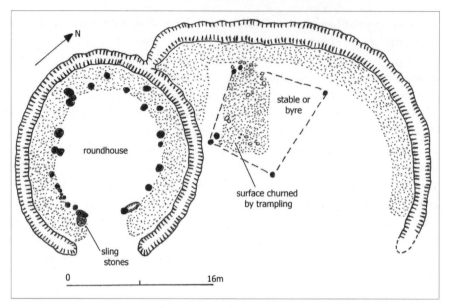

Iron Age roundhouse with its associated farming enclosure at Hod Hill, Dorset. The ditched yard contained a stable or cattle byre. (*I. A. Richmond*)

fields or dumped into the cattle byres along with old straw bedding and the dried rushes that were used to cover the house floor. Modern tribes who use roundhouses often mark out a spot for refuse disposal, typically in front of the door, but rarely any closer than 10 metres. The 'yard' area is routinely swept clean, creating a cleared arc of ground in front of the doorway. One study found that material swept away accumulated against the outer wall of the house, in ditches and hollows in the ground, and away from the door against fences or other obstacles.

The Modern Experience

Although I cannot in any way claim to have recreated the life of an Iron Age farmer, I have been lucky enough to spend several weekends inside Ryedale Folk Museum's roundhouse along with three colleagues. Ordinarily the house is quite sparsely furnished, a central hearth is flanked by two benches, two timber beds at the rear use straw as their mattresses, and to the left of the doorway (as one enters the house) is a rotary quern stone and a vertical weaving loom. Visitors rarely see the fire lit, with the result that the house appears cold, empty, and dark. Our aim was to furnish the house and spend two days and a night within it, cooking, eating and drinking, talking to the public, and then sleeping in the straw-filled beds.

It is interesting to compare our experiences with the archaeological evidence. Immediately we needed storage space, a place for the meat, vegetables, and other consumables that we had brought to cook. With the morning sun illuminating the 'work area' to the left of the doorway, we decided to place it in the periphery, against the outer wall to the right of the doorway. To conceal the stores from members of the public, we erected a heavy canvas screen around them, leaving access for ourselves at the rear. We threw deer and boar skins onto the beds along with undyed woollen blankets. Our spears, decorated shields, swords, and other Iron Age paraphernalia we decided to place in a prominent position so that visitors would not fail to be impressed by them. The best place seemed to be on the platforms that had been built over the beds as well as in the backspace—directly opposite the entrance to the roundhouse. By late morning the sun illuminated this area beautifully.

Our baskets, sacks, and farm tools were piled up against the outer wall, wherever there was space. The aim was to keep the central area around the hearth free of clutter since we would be spending much of our day there. A basket of charcoal and a large stack of firewood had to be close by, however, and so it was decided to put it along the front of the hearth, well out of the way. With sunlight streaming in through the entrance it seemed natural to sit in a horseshoe shape around the fire, facing both the light and any visitors who should enter. Tools, knives, chopping boards, bowls, and cups were stacked on handy tree stumps that served as low tables, or were stuffed underneath or just behind the benches. In this way they were always within reach, and being so close to hand meant that we didn't have to fumble through bags or baskets in the darkness at the back of the house to search for them.

The Iron Age house at Ryedale Folk Museum has a Celtic-style firedog over the hearth, which is an iron frame that stands over the fire. The bar across the top rotates and can be used as a spit, but we also found it extremely useful as a device from which to hang copper and iron pots, using small iron 'S' hooks. A jar of water was also kept by the fireside in case of accidents and also as a source of fresh water for cooking and drinking. Cutting up meat and vegetables was done on an oak chopping board that rested on top of a tree stump that we placed close to the fire. One problem that modern cooks rarely have to deal with is lack of light. This becomes apparent when trying to decide if meat is cooked, for example, or if stews are ready.

As the afternoon wore on, the light tracked across the back of the roundhouse until it faded and we closed the door. Although we would have liked to light lard-filled Iron Age lamps, the danger of knocking one over and setting fire to a sheepskin or bed was far too great. Instead we lit candles that were placed in glass jars and these we placed on the floor around the hearth around which we sat. Licks of flame from both the hearth and the flickering candles provided enough light to see faces and shadows cast on the walls, but darkness blanketed the recesses of the house. When we retired to bed the fire was sensibly damped down. Under blankets and on layers of straw and deerskin, we all slept well. One other resident was a mouse (plus family tucked away somewhere close by, no doubt), which must have survived off of the wheat grains scattered around the grindstone. This feature of the roundhouse is used by the museum with parties of school children. Hungry mice would have been a feature of every prehistoric house, I am sure. On one morning, in late August, the fierce summer sunrise shone through gaps in the doorway to illuminate my bed and bathe me in light, waking me suddenly at five o'clock in the morning. It was a glorious way to start the day and coincided with the calls of the museum's two competing cockerels.

In our experience, the roundhouse was warm and comfortable. During one weekend rain lashed the site, but the thatch proved up to the job and the house remained dry. We had some misgivings about a gap left by the builders between the top of the outer wall and the thatched roof, which (supported by an internal ring of posts) passed over it without touching. Wind and rain, however, did not penetrate this gap and it did indeed serve to let in light throughout the morning.

Finally, it is interesting to note how the circular form of the building drew all activities and attention towards the fire. It created a distinctly communal feel. Today the focal point in most of our post-modern homes is the corner of a room or a wall, and associated with a flat-screen television or a games console. Family members tend to face the same general direction. Spending time inside a reconstructed roundhouse has given us an appreciation of how all of the indoor activities are naturally orientated around the centre of the building. It provided us with a very different sense of living space. Perhaps the few modern experiences that compare would be that of a yacht's cabin with berths, where all is centred round the galley table.

7

Open-Fire Cooking

Near at hand are their fireplaces heaped with coals and on them are cauldrons and spits holding whole pieces of meat.

Diodorus Siculus 28

Fire provided three essentials for prehistoric folk: light, heat and the ability to cook food. Pot cookery, something with which we are very well acquainted with today, is discussed in a later chapter. It has similarities to the modern 'stove top' method of cooking, but with a number of marked differences. Some foods were simply not suitable or of small enough size to drop into a cookpot and so they were cooked directly on the fire itself, either over the flames, or in the embers.

The famous French chef Marcel Boulestin once claimed that 'cookery is not chemistry. It is an art'. However, in an age of exact measures, of controllable gas flames and oven timers, this is no longer the case. Cookery is science—it really is chemistry. Going back to an open wood fire, though, to the oldest technique of all, cooking is brought fully into the realm of art. Fire is unpredictable and there are innumerable variations that may affect the cooking process: the type of wood, for how long the wood was seasoned, how far from the fire the food is suspended, cooking over flame, or cooking over embers, the strength of the wind, and so on. The ability to read the fire, to make changes and to have some control over its heat and capricious nature, adds an ancient ring of truth to Boulestin's remark.

Many of the experiments for this book were carried out on the hearth within Ryedale Folk Museum's Iron Age roundhouse. Other techniques were practiced over a variety of other fires and fire pits over the last few years. A well-excavated hearth from a roundhouse near Battlesbury Camp hill fort provided a model for several of my cooking pits. The rectangular hearth at the centre of this Iron Age house was 15 cm deep and measured 90 cm × 60 cm. It featured a short extension from its south-east corner, which was either some kind of flue or (more likely) a cooking area that would have contained a bed of embers raked across from the main fire.

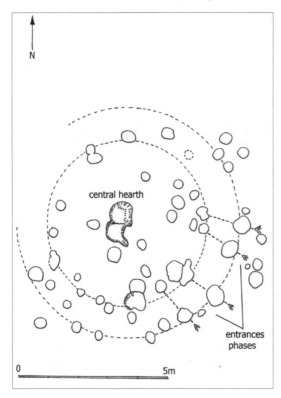

central hearth

entrances
phases

0   5m

Roundhouse of the Middle
Iron Age excavated at
Battlesbury Camp hill fort,
Wiltshire. The central hearth
was formed of two pits, cut
at different depths, with an
extension (or flue) extending
away toward the south-east.
(*S. E. James*)

Fire Lighting

Firewood must have been cut and stored during the winter months, giving
it a chance to dry out. This seasoned wood will then have burned well. As is
common in developing nations today, children will have foraged for sticks and
twigs throughout the year in order to eke out the family's store of firewood. In
general, softwoods (lime, willow, birch, and poplar) burn quickly and brightly,
while the native hardwoods (beech, ash, elm, and oak) are longer lasting and
tend to produce very hot embers. Yet each type of wood has its own qualities:

Alder: Burns quickly, although it is easy to light and is very good for
        smoking food.

Apple: Like cherry, apple wood is perfect for smoking and grilling food
        over the fire. Its aroma translates into flavour.

Ash: This burns slowly, but steadily and produces both bright flames
        and embers perfect for cooking.

Beech: Beech wood also burns slowly and is more difficult to light, but it does give off a lot of heat. Its flames are bright and its embers long lasting.

Birch: With hot, bright flames birch wood makes an ideal cooking fuel. It burns even when fresh and unseasoned, produces heat and, with its fragrant aroma, is ideal when food has to be smoked.

Gorse: The small branches of gorse burn easily and produce a lot of heat quite quickly. Gorse does not produce sparks.

Lime: Lime wood produces pleasant enough flames and is fairly flammable, although it gives off little heat.

Oak: Flames from oak are hot, although not very bright and burn slowly over a long period to produce useful embers. Oak wood can, however, be difficult (and frustrating) to light.

Pine: This wood can produce sparks and it produces quite a lot of soot. However, pine burns well and with a vivid flame.

Poplar: Poplar wood does not give off much heat, but burns brightly. It is very flammable, making it a good choice as a fire-lighter.

Willow: This wood makes poor fuel for a cooking fire, it burns poorly and produces few embers. On the upside, it creates very little smoke.

With the start of the Iron Age, fires could be lit by striking a piece of flint with a small length of steel. The sharp flint carves off a red-hot splinter of steel (the spark), which must be caught within a pile of tinder. I've used various types of tinder, including dried bracket fungus and charcloth, which is essentially 'cooked linen'. Charcloth catches a spark easily and after the glowing cloth is nested inside a large handful of dry grass, can be wafted and blown on until a flame ignites. Prior to the Iron Age, a nodule of iron pyrites would have served the same purpose. Other early fire-making techniques include the fire bow and the fire plough. The former uses a hardwood spindle, rotated by a small bow and bowstring. Spun in place on a softwood base, the spindle drills through the wood and (with both patience and luck) will ignite a small pile of tinder. The fire plough also uses the friction of a hardwood shaft on a softwood base, this time using a simple backwards and forwards motion along a groove cut into the base. Both require skill and determination to use effectively.

We should not assume that the roundhouse hearth required a fire starting every morning, though. It is easy to dig into the ashes of the hearth at sunrise to find a few glowing embers. The addition of a little tinder and some patient blowing will almost always bring yesterday's fire back to life. Ötzi the Ice Man was discovered in the Italian Alps along with all of his equipment; this included a small birch bark container, blackened on the inside, that probably held a piece of glowing bracket fungus. Carried in this way, the smouldering ember could be carried some distance and then used to start a new fire.

Over the Flames

Spit Roasting

It seems that the usual way of roasting fowl or large joints of meat was by turning on a spit over the fire. For most of the period the spit would have been a straight green bough, hopefully with a natural 'crank' at one end, that rested on two upright and Y-shaped (or forked) branches. In the Iron Age, however, elaborate firedogs were the fashion. These were iron stands in the shape of a single crossbar, close to the floor, that ended in a pair of upright pillars often topped with elegantly wrought animal heads. It is thought that the firedog served several purposes, the bar along the floor probably supporting firewood in the hearth, while a second bar spanning the gap from animal head to animal head, served as a spit. In our own work with an Iron Age firedog, the spit saw use both as a method to slow roast meat, but also as a pot hanger.

Of course, even in the metal-rich world of the Iron Age, sinking that much iron into a single item would have been a great expenditure. Yet the firedog sat in the hearth, at the centre of the roundhouse, the focus of social life and something all visitors will have seen and admired. In the great and noble houses throughout history, the job of squatting by the fire and continuously rotating the spit was given to a slave or servant known as a turnspit. Modern electric rotisseries replace this drudgery, but in fact constant rotation of the spit is not absolutely necessary.

Spit roasting is the most effective way of cooking large fatty or cylindrical-shaped foods, including whole birds, lamb legs, pork loins, and of course whole pig, lamb, or goat. The process will require several hours during which the cook must attend both to the rotation of the spit (which ensures even cooking) and also the fire. Prior to threading the iron spit through the meat, it may necessary to first tie up a roast or bird with either wet string or fresh cordage, in order to keep it compact and symmetrical. Wooden skewers can also be used to impale the joint which pass through a hole that has been bored into the spit itself. Without these measures a poorly mounted piece of meat may not turn at all, but simply hang over the fire, the spit rotating futilely through its centre. Smaller animals such as squirrel or hare, (once gutted) will instead need to be laid onto the spit with legs tied together.

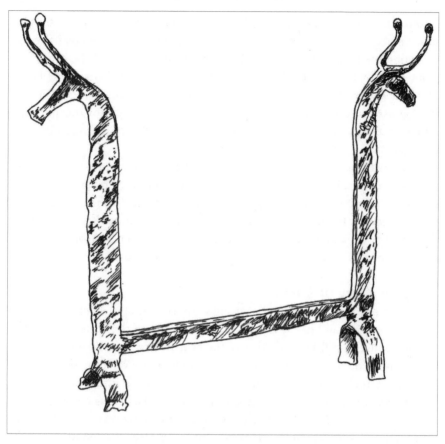

Iron firedogs from Lords Bridge, Barton, Cambridgeshire. This utilitarian kitchen furniture actually formed the centrepiece of any wealthy roundhouse family.

Hardwoods are needed as fuel for this type of roasting, and the fire should be lit at least one hour before the meat goes into the spit. The rule of thumb when building an effective fire for spit roasting is that the embers should provide a moderate level of heat. To test this, the cook should be able to hold his hand over the embers at the level of the spit for at least three seconds. Once the meat is roasting over the embers the spit can be turned a little at a time, and a strategically placed stick used to lock the crank end in place. By slowly turning the spit incrementally and the careful positioning of coals beneath the spit, the meat can be slowly and evenly roasted.

Our own spit roasting concentrated on poultry, and at no time did we employ a drip tray. This is something recommended by most modern cooks, since the juices that run out of the cooking meat can be used to make a delicious gravy—they should not be wasted. However, we lacked a suitable prehistoric container in which to catch the juices and had to let them drip into the hearth. Locating the firedog at the front of the hearth is a sensible move since it gives the cook more control of the heat. A central fire can be maintained near the back and hot embers pulled toward the spit at the front as and when needed. Fresh fuel will be added to the back of the fire so that it does not interfere with the spit and the bed of embers below it. The firedog used in our own experiments was a little too high for our purposes and so required a strong fire with flames in order to adequately cook the roast.

One advantage of the spit roast process is the opportunity to smoke the meat as it cooks. Hardwood chips can be tossed into the embers at frequent intervals, creating smoke that adds additional flavour to the turning meat. Since the idea is to create smoke and not to simply burn up these woodchips, they must be soaked in water for an hour or two prior to use. Aromatic woods are ideal for this process such as cherry, apple, alder, or oak.

Hanging a Leg of Lamb

Some cuts of meat are simply the wrong shape for the spit. A leg of lamb, for example, is wide and heavy at one end, narrowing to the bone at the other, yet the joint can still be roasted over the hearth. The trick is to suspend the leg of lamb from a wooden tripod, using strong twine. With the bone serving as a strong anchor point, the joint can be easily hoisted into a position over the embers and it will spin with little provocation. The heat is most intense at the widest part of the joint while the slender end faces away from the coals, thus receiving a lot less heat. Of course this is a perfect combination and the narrow end of the leg of lamb should be cooked through by the time the bulk of the meat is ready. The tripod may simply be formed from three poles lashed together, each one roughly the height of a man. All of the advice given for spit roasting is pertinent here; carefully manage the fire and the coal bed to ensure the meat receives as much heat as needed, but no more and no less.

Grilled Fish in Cages

As on any modern barbeque, fish can be grilled quickly over a wood fire. If small, the fish can simply be skewered lengthways with a single green branch and then propped over the fire, but a more efficient method is to bind it within a cage of pliable branches. The cage is simply made using three parallel lengths of willow with two or three cross-beams then lashed on using strips of willow bark. After the fish is laid on to the cross beams, additional lengths of willow are woven in to trap it within the cage. At the Ryedale roundhouse we leaned the fish cages against the firedog and there our gutted mackerel cooked nicely.

In the Ashes

As anyone familiar with good barbeque practice will know, cooking does not rely on flame, but on heat. The embers and ashes that remain after a wood fire has burnt down will retain enough heat with which to continue cooking. Embers are the glowing coals of burnt wood and are hot enough to grill clay-baked food and steaks directly, while ash is the powdery residue left once carbon is burnt off. An ash bed in the hearth can be used to bake eggs and ash cakes.

Steak in Embers

Beef steak, like other thick cuts of meat, can be cooked directly on a bed of embers. The embers should be flattened ready to receive the steak, and should not be glowing red—let them cool a little (they will quickly fade to black). The steak will require turning once or twice with a knife or sharp stick. Inevitably hot coals will stick to the underside of the steak, but these can be quickly cleaned off using a clean stick or a knife, before placing it back onto the embers.

Roast Egg

Eggs are a perfect dish for an ash bed, primarily because each egg comes with its own miniature cook pot—the shell. Our own experiments have included quail, hen, duck, and goose eggs—all with fairly tasty results. Of course, in a manner similar to roasting chestnuts, the roast egg must first have its shell pierced (at the top) to prevent an unsightly explosion later on. It took a number of attempts to perfect the roast egg. As it sits in the ashes (and especially in the dark of a roundhouse) it is difficult to judge the point at which the egg is done. The brilliance of the roast egg is that it requires neither pot nor boiling water. The handy 'pot cloth' that is kept beside any prehistoric fire for turning pots, lifting metal handles, or revolving hot iron spits, is the perfect tool for plucking well-done eggs from the ashes.

Ash Cake

American pioneers and Australian stockmen alike baked bread in the ashes of their camp fires. Thousands of years before, Babylonian soldiers boasted of their rough and ready existence, and their reliance on these 'flat loaves in ashes', as recorded in the Epic of Erra [1.57]:

> *For real men, going off to war,*
> *It's a feast! ...*
> *The best bread from the city [leavened and raised]*
> *Cannot match the bread baked under ashes!*
> *The sweetest beer*
> *Cannot match the water from a flask!*

This field expedient form of baking was popular with both soldiers and nomads in the ancient world and, in the Roman era, ash cakes were known as *panis focacius*. The Latin term *focus* meant 'hearth'—these were loaves baked in the ashes of the hearth, a tradition that survived the fall of the Roman Empire. Today, aficionados of Italian cookery can enjoy the modern descendant of the *panis focacius*, the flat bread we know as *focaccia*.

The beauty of baking in the ashes was its simplicity; no cook pots or portable ovens were needed and the only ingredients were flour, water, and salt. Once the dough is made it is placed directly into the ashes; because of this, hardwoods are probably best used since they do not contain the resins present in most softwoods—resins that can pass their flavour onto the bread. A 1946 edition of the *Sydney Morning Herald* related the Australian bushman's method for cooking ash cakes, known nationally as 'dampers' after the practice of damping down the fire with a spade-full of ash:

> Take 1 lb of flour, water and a pinch of salt. Mix it into a stiff dough and knead for at least one hour, not continuously, but the longer it is kneaded the better the damper. Press with the hands into a flat cake and cook it in at least a foot of hot ashes.

I have not followed these instructions exactly, but they do indicate how simple the procedure is. Take spelt flour and a pinch of salt and then add water until it has the texture you need—if too sticky then add flour, if too dry then add water, then knead for ten minutes. Place the dough carefully onto a flattened area of hot ashes and then cover the damper with a shovelful of ashes. Baking time varies with the size of the damper, but to check it, brush away the topmost ashes; a quick finger flick will ring hollow if done. Continue brushing off the ashes (use a leafy twig or handful of grasses) and then use a shovel or short plank of wood to lift the damper out of the hearth. With a knife winkle out any embers or pieces of charcoal that are still adhering to the base of the crust. It doesn't look very appetising, but slice the damper and you will (hopefully) reveal a moist and well-baked bread.

Oysters in Shells

Oysters were popular with the Romans after the invasion, but these shellfish were also eaten by the prehistoric Britons. They are extremely easy to cook in the embers; simply arrange them, rounded side facing down, on a very shallow bed of coals. Not much heat is required to successfully cook these shellfish. After the shells open, they are edible, although most diners will want to wait a little longer (unless they like their oysters rare). Do not wait too long, however, since the oysters will continue to cook and while they cook they will shrink and eventually dry out altogether. Lift the oysters out of the embers and then use a knife to prise off the top shell. Using the knife once again, slide the blade underneath the meat and lift it from the oyster shell. Eat while hot.

Clay-Baked Food

Several types of food can be cooked within the embers of a fire, as long as the food is protected against the fierce heat and contamination from the ash. Coating the item in clay is a wonderful way to cook and it is not simply a 'needs must' method of last resort cookery. Clay baking brings with it the unique advantage of 'locking in' the food's juices and flavours—they simply cannot escape. Misshapen and poorly fired lumps of clay are common finds on prehistoric sites and clay baking is one of the most plausible interpretations for them.

I have carried out several clay-bake experiments with great success. Clay from the cliffs at Speeton, on the North Yorkshire coast, was used for the purpose. Thin sheets of clay are prepared and then, one by one, wrapped around the item to be cooked. The sheets of clay are joined together both by smoothing and the addition of extra pieces of clay, until the entire item is covered. Any areas of thin clay should be strengthened and the finished product placed on a piece of wood to dry next to the fire. Remember to turn it once or twice so that the clay coating dries evenly. Once dry, the clay-baked food can be placed into the hearth; ashes and embers must then be piled both around and on top of it.

When the food is ready (again this will depend on what is being cooked, but half an hour to forty-five minutes should suffice for most dishes) the clay casing is removed from the fire and placed back on its wooden tray. I use an iron hammer (or simple Neolithic-style hammer stone) to crack open the clay and reveal the food within. Alternatively, crack the casing with the hammer and then tease the clay away with a knife. Quickly, the cooked meat within is revealed and can be placed onto a serving plate. Just be careful to remove any pieces of baked clay still adhering. Whether cooking fish, lamb, or poultry, the meat should be full of flavour since the clay casing has prevented juices from either boiling or leaking away. Clay baking is best suited to small pieces of meat rather than large joints, which are instead dealt with using an earth oven (described in Chapter 11).

Our first experiments with clay baking fish were not entirely successful. Armed with half-a-dozen trout one weekend in 2008, we proposed to try a couple of different cooking methods. My colleague, Jamie, and I went about it in two different ways; although we had conducted only the barest of research, we really did want to experiment and see what we could come up with on our own. I carefully and completely coated two gutted trout in fresh clay. These I laid out in the sun for a couple of hours in order to dry out. We had decided that the clay would need to be placed onto the fire as dry as possible to allow the heat to pass through to the fish within. Jamie also wanted to experiment with a method of cooking using direct heat; he wanted to spit roast the fish.

We prepared our fire and then spread out the coals. My two ready prepared trout-in-clay went onto the coals and I piled additional embers on top of them. We decided to wait around half an hour before cracking open the clay jackets. Meanwhile, Jamie skewered his trout with two green stakes, feeding each sharpened stick in and out along the length of the fish. It didn't look solid. We realised quite quickly that many more sticks would really be needed to support the weight of the fish. It was too late to fashion more skewers from greenwood, however, so we persevered with the technique. As the fish cooked on the skewers, the inevitable happened, the flesh became soft, the head drooped and most of the trout fell into the fire. In our defence we had predicted this turn of events, so it was not a shock. Our remaining trout was placed directly onto a low bed of embers. Could this simple method deliver us a well-cooked fish? The naked trout began to cook instantly, but as soon as we began to move it, the fish became too badly fouled with ashes to open and eat—we abandoned that one too.

Feeling a bit like the first men to discover fire, fumbling and failing with different methods of cooking our fish, we turned to the two trout that we had coated in clay jackets. How would these fare? It was time to take my clay-covered trout out of the fire and to do this I used a sturdy stick and a thin batten of wood as a tray. Both clay-baked fish came out of the fire well and were ready to crack open. The back of an axe made short work of the fire-hardened clay and as I gently peeled chunks of it away, we were amazed to find that it brought the fish skin with it, revealing pink, perfectly cooked, trout meat. However, although the meat was well-cooked on top, it was a little raw underneath. The second clay-baked fish that Jamie opened must have been well-covered with embers because it was perfectly cooked throughout. Both fish tasted delicious and were extremely juicy—we surmised that the baked clay had sealed in the juices during cooking.

Trout in Clay:
The whole fish, gutted, but with tail and head intact, can be used. Stuff the trout with butter and chopped ramson bulbs (or spring onions) and sprinkle with salt. Coat with clay and leave to dry next to the fire before baking in the embers for half an hour. As the fired clay comes away it will pull the skin of the fish with it, revealing within the juicy pink flesh and cooked ramsons within. This dish has been a sure-fire success every time.

Wild Bird in Clay:
Just as the baked clay takes fish skin away with it, the feathers of a wild bird will come away just the same. Hunters throughout prehistory may have used this speedy cooking technique, particularly since it does away with cook pots

Early Bronze Age Beaker kit, including ash bow, wrist bracer, copper dagger, bone belt buckle, and a red deer quiver, based on the example found with Ötzi, the Ice Man. Clothing is based on remains found in Danish burials.

Golden neck torcs, arm rings, and pendants from the Late Bronze Age, found in Wiltshire, England. These items of gold jewellery were worn to denote status within the tribe and, like bronze, gold was acquired through complex trade networks, which made it accessible only to the British chiefs and their families.

Iron Age farmers owed allegiance to a chief, and were called to war by him. Tunics and cloaks are made of wool and the shield motifs are taken from coins of the period

A Star Carr supper. Mesolithic hunter-gatherers had a wide array of food choices available to them. Here we have venison, beef (from wild cattle), mussels, oysters and razor shells, dandelion, hazelnuts, rose-hip berries, and beech nuts.

Reconstructed roundhouses based on Bronze Age ground plans. These turf-covered houses were built at the Flag Fen museum, near Peterborough.

Haystack at Pokhara, Nepal. These haystacks are built around a central pole and are typically raised above the ground on low timber platforms. Evidence suggests that prehistoric haystacks were also built around a central supporting pole.

The Soay is a tough, hardy sheep that resembles the wild ancestor of modern breeds. These Soay are kept at Flag Fen museum and represent the type of sheep kept by Bronze Age farmers.

Attempts to recreate the breed of pig farmed by Iron Age communities involved the cross-breeding of wild boar with the modern Tamworth pig.

Goats in Chitwan, southern Nepal. They are grazing on leafy twigs, hung up as fodder by the householder. Staff at Butser Ancient Farm likewise found that their goats were happy to graze on dried leaves.

Harvest time in the Iron Age.

Wearing Bronze Age clothing, the author repairs part of the roundhouse boundary—a wattle fence.

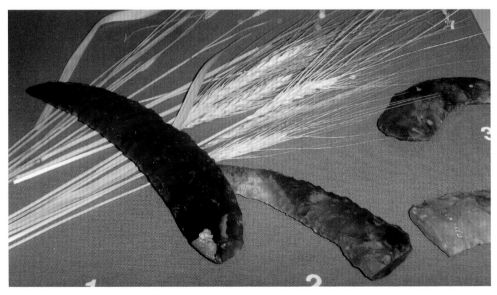

A collection of beautifully knapped flint sickles from the Late Neolithic. These examples are in the Hull and East Riding Museum.

Above: Reproduction of the copper axe carried by Ötzi, the Ice Man.

Below: Replica prehistoric axes and blades. Across the top is a Ewart Park-style sword. Below, from left to right, are an (original) Neolithic stone axehead from Marton in East Yorkshire, a copper axehead, a copy of a bronze flat axe from Butterwick in North Yorkshire, a copper dagger from the Roundway G8 barrow in Wiltshire, and, on the right, an Areton Down-style dagger blade.

Above: Bronze Age belongings—2300 BC. A grooved ware cookpot sits behind one of the new Bell Beaker drinking cups. Other items include green malachite (copper ore), a birch bark container, gold basket earrings, a fish hook, arrowhead, and decorative sun disk. Amber sits next to a piece of pine resin that will be used to glue flint heads onto arrows. Tools include a flat axe, awl, pressure flaker, and two flint knives—one with wooden handle, the other mounted on a bone handle.

Below: The Iron Age roundhouse at Ryedale Folk Museum, in North Yorkshire. Built in 2006, it is based on a house plan excavated at a quarry in nearby Pickering.

Inside the roundhouse at midday in summer. Light streams in from the door, yet the interior is still quite dark. A water jug sits by the fire and two copper pans hang from the cross beam of the iron firedog.

A cattle byre in central Nepal. Similar structures (although round in shape) are frequent finds near prehistoric roundhouses.

John strips bark from willow branches ready to make cages in which we will roast our fish. We found that the porch of the roundhouse makes an ideal work area, providing shade from sun or wind and providing a wall to lean on.

Duck roasts on the iron spit, while a lamb stew bubbles in the copper pan behind it. Shields and other accoutrements are leant against the back wall and you may notice that the wall itself does not quite meet the thatched roof, allowing light to enter.

Mackerel cook over the fire. Simple interwoven cages were fashioned from fresh willow branches and then leant against the iron firedog that sat across the hearth.

Ash cake, a simple bread made of flour and water baked in the ashes of the hearth. Although the crust is burnt, the interior is well-baked and edible.

Stuffed lambs hearts. Once stuffed with mushroom, chives, breadcrumbs, and ground hazelnuts, these hearts were then coated in clay and cooked in the embers of the hearth.

Piles of carbonised chestnut shells are common finds on prehistoric sites, from the Mesolithic to the Iron Age. We roasted the nuts by putting them in a shallow pit, over which we lit a fire.

Using an Iron Age rotary quern, Jamie rocks the top stone through 90 degrees in order to grind wheat grains. A saddle quern, used during the Neolithic and Bronze Ages, sits just behind him.

Prehistoric flatbreads, from left to right: malted wheat bread, spelt bread, and flax bread.

Bronze Age pottery including a collared urn (left), Bell Beaker (centre) and food vessel (right).

A colourful springtime soup that boasts all of the colour and flavour of early spring blooms. Ingredients can vary; this soup contains dandelion, chives, ground ivy, red deadnettle, gorse flowers, hawthorn leaves, and a little Jack-in-the-Hedge, all cooked in butter.

Smoky stew, a dish of smoked fish, smoked bacon, chives, and gorse flowers fried in butter and then cooked in milk.

Beef and beer stew, with mushrooms and Jack-in-the-Hedge. This is a fragrant plant that adds tones of garlic and mustard to the dish; it is best added at the very end of the cooking process.

Cooking pork in an earth oven. The joints have been covered in a protective coat of dough before being placed into the stone-lined fire pit. It was then covered over with more hot stones, turf, and soil for two hours.

Pork joint freshly dug out of the earth oven. It was cooked well, right through to the centre. Note the baked crust that has protected the meat.

and pans, requiring instead only a few handfuls of river clay. The bird could have been gutted, cooked, and eaten easily on the trail. Bones of teal, swan, goose, widgeon, woodcock, and plover have all been discovered at prehistoric sites in Britain and a number of seabird species, including puffin, guillemot, and gannet have been found within wheelhouses on the Hebridean island of North Uist.

Stuffed Heart in Clay:
A stuffing made of bread crumbs, mushrooms, mint leaves, and crushed hazelnuts is seasoned with a little sea salt. A lamb's heart is prepared; first remove any unwanted gristle and then with thumb and forefinger push into the openings to expand the chambers inside. This done, fill with the stuffing and then coat with clay. Be warned, the hearts do not take long to bake and are easily burnt. Surprisingly, the heart resembles lamb meat in both texture and flavour. A very tasty dish.

Under the Fire

One extremely simple cooking technique involves building a fire directly over the food. This requires no utensils, no water, and no cook pot. For mobile groups, like Mesolithic hunter-gatherers, this type of cooking is extremely attractive. During the Vietnam War, the Viet Cong guerrillas who found themselves out on long-range patrols would carry with them a ration of dried rice. To cook it they would wrap the rice in cloth and soak it in water. When swollen, the fighters were then able to bury it just under the surface of the ground. A fire was lit above it and the heat, radiating downwards, would cook the rice. This ingenuity may have been shared by the Mesolithic Britons who had no cook pots and needed to cook their food while on the trail or the beach, or while out foraging. Obviously most foods would be burnt beyond recognition if cooked in this way, but some, like nuts and shellfish, are actually protected by their own fireproof case.

Hazelnuts in Shells
Evidence from many prehistoric sites across northern Europe suggests that hazelnuts were often cooked in this manner. When replicating the technique I dug a shallow, bowl-shaped hollow and spread a layer of beach sand on to it. Next, thirty or forty hazelnuts were scattered into the pit and gently pressed into the sand.

After covering the nuts with soil a fire was built above the depression and left to burn slowly for around an hour. Once the fire had died down it was raked away and the soil dug up to reveal charred hazelnuts. The most challenging part of the exercise was digging all of the nuts out of the sand without leaving any behind. All the nuts had softened in their shells and carried with them a mild toasted flavour. Cooked this way, the hazelnuts proved to be extremely edible and they were soon consumed by everyone who had helped in the enterprise.

Mussels in Shells

Fried or boiled mussels are familiar to us today, but it is simpler and more evocative of the Mesolithic age to bake them beneath a fierce, but fast-burning brushwood fire. Since the mussels are best cooked while they are standing upright, the first step is to place a small stone at the centre of the cooking area. Lean one mussel up against it, with the pointed end sticking upward. Continue to lean mussels around this stone and then around the first layer of mussels, continue stacking the mussels in a concentric manner, all leaning in toward that central stone.

Once this elaborate sculpture of marine dominoes is complete, gently place brushwood on top. Use fast-burning twigs, or even pine needles, which are dry and flammable and which fall down between the shells. Light the fuel and let the fire burn itself out (it should only take a few minutes). Dig out all the mussels and eat all those whose shells have opened. There may have been some cooler spots in the fire where a cluster of shells failed to open, in this case gather them together and immediately repeat the process. Any that fail to open during this second baking should be discarded.

Limpets in Shells

I cooked limpets on my local beach and found them to be edible, though with the sea-salt chewiness of calamari. Limpets, unlike hand-gathered mussels, are almost always safe to eat. Collecting these 'fruits of the sea' can be troublesome however; limpets, as the name suggest, remain stubbornly attached to the rock. The best technique to use is to find a pebble on the shoreline that is long and thin, but that still carries some weight. I suppose a stout piece of wood will serve just as well. Creeping up on the stationary limpets, try to swing the stone briskly sideways to knock them clean off the stone.

Once a dozen or so have been collected, sit them together on a flat rock with their protective shells facing upwards, as nature intended. A few large handfuls of brushwood are then piled on top of the limpets and ignited, burning for around ten minutes. It is a simple matter to then sweep the ashes away and lift the shells off of the cooked limpets. The meat of each shellfish will remain behind and does not look particularly appetising, topped as it is with a black blister. This must be plucked off and discarded. The small disc of meat that is left can be eaten. Baked limpet is certainly not a gourmet food, but for hunter-gatherers, or agriculturalists that are perhaps faced with a poor harvest, they are easy to gather, plentiful, and nutritious.

8

DAIRY FOODS

From milk is also made butter, among barbarian tribes accounted the choicest food, one that distinguishes the richer from the lower orders.

Pliny, *Natural History*, 28.35

The tribes of northern Europe, the Celts and the Germans, were noted by writers like Tacitus, Pliny, and Julius Caesar as milk producers. In this they were rather unusual in the ancient world. Intolerance to lactose seems to be an in-built evolutionary trait among adult mammals that prevents healthy young from remaining dependant on their mothers. Certain cultures have, over time, become lactose tolerant, the tribes of northern Europe included. It is not hard to see why. With a limited growing season in these northerly climes, it made sense to exploit the food source of animal milk if it could be tolerated. Over time, entire communities were able to consume milk and bring the production of dairy foods into the farming economy.

Fresh milk may have been drunk in small quantities, but in an age without pasteurisation, its storage or transport was impractical. Milk is an excellent medium for the growth of harmful bacteria that can lead to severe stomach illness and even death. Salmonella, tuberculosis (*mycobacterium bovis*), listeria, and other bacteria are all able to develop successfully within unpasteurised milk. Both butter and cheese-making are techniques used to extend its life.

Cream

A number of food types can be made from raw milk and the easiest of these to produce is cream. Left alone to stand, milk naturally separates into cream and the low-fat milk that it has left behind. Since the fat in cream is less dense it rises to the top from where it can be skimmed off. Clotted or scalded cream is a favourite of West Country tea rooms today and since it has a slightly longer shelf-life, may have also been popular with prehistoric communities. Another benefit of heating up the milk to near boiling temperatures is the possibility of killing off some of the harmful bacteria that make raw milk their home.

Clotted Cream

While the milk is still warm from the cow, pour it into the widest cooking pot you have and leave this to stand overnight. In the morning the cream will have separated and risen to the top of the pot. Do not stir or otherwise disturb the pot of milk and cream as you carry it to the fire. Now warm it very slowly and very gently in the embers of the hearth. The milk should remain over the heat until it is very hot, but do not let it boil or you will end up with a skin instead of cream. You may need to stir the cream gently in order to stop it scorching or sticking to the sides of the pan. An hour or so should suffice—this will vary depending on the amount of milk, the size of the pot, and the heat given off by the coal bed—the slower the scalding is done the better. Thick undulations should appear on the surface when it is ready and once this stage is reached remove the pot from the heat and let it stand overnight once again. In the morning simply scoop the clotted or scalded cream from the top of the pot. Do not waste the low-fat milk left behind, the roundhouse cook would never have wasted food and it can be put to use in other recipes.

Sour Cream

When it is allowed to stand at room temperature, cream will naturally ferment and thicken; it becomes more acidic, which passes a mild sour taste on to the cream. How long this takes depends on the weather. During the summer it is possible to pour the cream out into a deep pan in the early evening and then wake up to find sour cream the following morning. During the colder, winter months, however, you will have to ripen your cream next to the hearth, remembering to turn the pot occasionally to ensure that the heat reaches the cream evenly.

Of course, sour cream produced in this way will last a little longer than raw milk. Since cream will have been collected from several days' worth of milking, the prehistoric cook will have discovered that it had begun to naturally ferment. This fermented sour cream acts as the basic ingredient for making butter. Today we call butter made from sour milk 'cultured butter' and the butter derived from pasteurised milk, 'sweet cream butter'. It is the latter form of butter that is popular in Britain and the USA.

Sweet Cream Pudding

While most cooks in the West employ sour cream as an accompaniment, using it to flavour other foods, the Norwegians have incorporated it into a traditional porridge recipe called Rømmegrøt. The sweet cream pudding described below is inspired by the Norwegian Christmas dish:

- 1 litre sour cream
- Around 200 g flour (to thicken)
- One cup of warm milk
- 50 g honey
- 25 g butter

Simmer the sour cream for about fifteen minutes. Next, sprinkle in some of the flour and stir. Keep adding flour in this way until the mixture reaches the consistency of good porridge. Continue to simmer, stirring occasionally to prevent the pudding from sticking to the pot. Skim off any butter fat that rises to the surface.

While the milk is warmed in a second pot over the fire, increase the heat beneath the pudding and bring it to the boil. At this point begin adding in the hot milk to thin out the sweet cream pudding. Whisk until smooth and then simmer gently for a further ten minutes. Finally, add the honey and melted butter and serve. This is a sweet, rich dish and the Norwegians traditionally eat it with cured meats.

Butter

In ancient Greece and Rome, the barbarians of Europe were renowned for their eccentric habits, such as wearing trousers and eating butter. In one of his plays, the Greek poet Anaxandrides (quoted by Athenaeus) calls the Thracians of Eastern Europe '*boutyphagoi*', or 'butter-eaters'. Pliny tells us that among the northern tribes, butter was made mostly from cow's milk, although the richest came from sheep and goat. Milk and milk products had been a staple food of northern Europe since the domestication of cattle. This emphasis on dairy foods rather than olive oil clearly distinguished the Celtic from the Roman diet. For the Romans, butter was simply a base for ointments and salves, not something in which you cooked your food.

Pliny's comment from the start of the chapter, that butter distinguished the rich from the poor, does suggest that the process to make it was difficult and time consuming. However, butter can be made quite easily without recourse to elaborate equipment or ingredients. He goes on to describe a method that he has heard about:

In winter the milk is warmed, while in summer the butter is extracted merely by shaking it rapidly in a tall vessel. This has a small hole to admit the air, made just under the mouth, which is otherwise completely stopped. There is added a little water to make the milk turn sour. The part that curdles most, floating on the top, is skimmed off ... what comes to the surface is butter, a fatty substance. The stronger the taste, the more highly is butter esteemed.

Pliny 28.35

The fats in milk or cream are normally prevented from coming together to form a single mass by membranes of emulsifiers around the fatty globules. Butter-making is the process of agitating the milk (or more usefully the cream) to break these membranes, allowing the fats to join up into a single mass. Shaking, beating, or churning are all ways in which this is achieved.

To make butter, put about 500 g of cream that has been ripened (or soured) into a bowl and whisk. Continue whisking until the cream begins to resemble scrambled eggs. Further thrashing of the cream will result in the solid butter separating out from the white buttermilk. It is an easy task to strain the buttermilk and remove the butter for washing. All traces of buttermilk have to be washed out of the butter, or else it will turn rancid over the next few days. Stir the butter in a bowl with a little fresh water, drain and repeat until the water runs clear. After adding a little salt, the butter should be ready for storage in a dark and relatively cool location.

A number of wooden casks, the earliest dated to the fifth century AD, have been found within Irish and Scottish peat bogs. Although now rancid and inedible, most of the barrels seem to have contained butter that was deposited in the anaerobic environment of the bogs where it would remain cool and fresh for great lengths of time. The largest casks of butter weighed as much as 18 kg. Other finds suggest that the practice of 'bog butter', however, was a much older one going back at least to the Iron Age. The Roman writer Tacitus reported:

[The German tribes] are wont also to dig out subterranean caves, and pile on them great heaps of dung, as a shelter from winter and as a receptacle for the year's produce, for by such places they mitigate the rigour of the cold. And should an enemy approach, he lays waste the open country, while what is hidden and buried is either not known to exist, or else escapes him from the very fact that it has to be searched for.

Tacitus, *Germania*, 16

In Britain, a type of mysterious subterranean rock-built structure called a *fogou* or *souterrain* has been discovered. These long and narrow hollows are typically associated either with the storage of food or as a place of defence. The words of Tacitus, above, suggest that in fact both uses can be ascribed to these manmade caves. Butter and cheese must have formed a large part of any such cold-store, but many other foods, from dried vegetables to salted meat, smoked fish and other supplies, must also have been kept there. The fact that not all Iron Age settlements had their own *fogou* could perhaps be explained by a statement made by the writer Strabo: 'some of [the British], though well supplied with milk, make no cheese' (Strabo 4.5).

Fresh Cheese

Cheese is yet another way in which milk can be turned into solid food. While butter-making liberates the fat content of the milk, cheese-making focusses instead on caseins that make up the bulk of its protein. By adding some form of acid to the milk, the caseins are forced to lump together to create white, chunky solids called curds, the prime constituent of cheese. The watery fluid left behind is still full of nutrients, but it is no longer milk, instead this by-product is known as whey. Whey, like most by-products was always put to use; it makes a nutritious drink on its own, or, as Cato recommended in his book *De Agricultura* [150.2], should be fed to pigs in order to help fatten them up.

It seems that the Germans ate cheese. Indeed, Tacitus remarks that their diet was simple, consisting of wild fruit, fresh game, and curdled milk. The Latin term used is *lac concretum,* a simple fresh cheese that is formed when milk is left to go sour of its own accord—the milk's own lactic acids doing the curdling. This type of fresh cheese has formed a part of European diet for centuries and survives today as the English cottage cheese, the northern European quark, and the Italian ricotta.

To accelerate the curdling process, heat can be applied and an acid added to the milk; in prehistoric Britain, beer will have served this purpose well.

Beer Cheese
- 1 litre full fat milk
- 250 ml brown ale
- Sprinkle of salt

Skimmed or low fat milk (that has perhaps had its cream skimmed off for some other use) can still be used for making fresh or soft cheese, but a whole milk will produce more solids during the curdling process. Heat the milk up in the pot until it is about to rise, at which point you should take it out of the hearth and pour in the beer. As you stir, the milk curds should appear almost immediately. I have found that warmed beer has an even speedier effect, although it is doubtful if it produces any more curds in the long run. Within just a few minutes the curds will have completely separated from the whey.

Place a linen cloth (I have a piece that I use solely for my cheese making) into a wide wooden bowl and then empty out the curds and whey into it. Next, carefully tie up the cloth and suspend it over the bowl from a beam in the roundhouse. It can be left overnight to drain and should be occasionally squeezed to force out any remaining whey. The resultant cheese will have retained a gentle flavour of beer and be crumbly and delicious. For those wanting a traditional curds-and-whey-style cottage cheese, do not squeeze the cheesecloth and let it hang for only an hour or so, before emptying the contents into a bowl. Soft cheese is best served with fresh bread.

Sour Cream Cheese

In this recipe, the sour cream acts as the acid, and takes the place of the brown ale. Use about 250 ml of sour cream, and follow the instructions given above for beer cheese.

Sweet Cheese

Tasty though both sour cream cheese and beer cheese are, they can be made into a sweet treat with the addition of honey, crushed hazelnuts, autumn berries, chopped mint, myrtle, or chive leaves. Again, follow the recipe for beer cheese, but as a final step, chop up the additional ingredients and gently fold them into the cheese. Leave suspended for an hour or so before serving.

Smoked Cheese

The inevitable result of hanging up the cheese-cloth from roundhouse rafters is the development of a faint smoky flavour. This effect can be accentuated by purposefully suspending the cheese cloth over a smoky hearth that is burning a sweet-smelling wood, perhaps oak chips or applewood, a fuel that the Roman agriculturalist, Columella, specifically recommended. Pliny suggested that smoking was a good way to improve the flavour of goat's cheese.

Hard Cheese

A hard cheese has been pressed and ripened over a period of time in a cool, dark place. French Roquefort cheese, for example, is still matured in the Combalou caves near Roquefort-sur-Soulzon, and as we have already seen, this type of subterranean storage was certainly employed by historic communities in northern Europe. Since ripening can take many months, milk can be transformed into cheese during a time of plenty and be eaten later in the year once it has ripened. Cheese ripening is a far more complex process than making fresh cheese, requiring rennet (an enzyme extracted from the stomach of a calf) as well as cheese presses. Often these types of cheeses are coated in wax or fat in order to properly seal them.

9

BAKING BREAD

At a small fishing village in Tanzania, on the shores of Lake Victoria, I was interested to see maize kernels (sweetcorn) drying in the sun both on blankets and on plastic sheets. I assumed this was a prelude to grinding in order to bake American-style cornbread. I was even more convinced when I was shown a communal petrol-powered corn mill, but I was wrong. My guide from the local Sukuma tribe, explained that the cornmeal produced at the little milling machine (protected by a tiny mud-brick building) would actually be used to make *ugali*, a thick porridge that is boiled until it reaches a heavy dough-like consistency. *Ugali* is the food of the poor who live around East Africa's great lakes, and it is most often broken into lumps and then dipped into sauce or stew, or it is wrapped around pieces of meat or vegetable to pluck them from the bowl. It is perfect finger food that is quick to make and unsophisticated, requiring neither yeast nor bread oven.

This one example goes to show that a simple farming or fishing community can exploit a source of carbohydrates (in this instance maize, but also wheat, rice, oats, barley, and so on) without relying on the need for a large bread oven. After the Roman invasion, domed-shaped ovens built of clay were common and they were used primarily for the baking of bread. Such ovens continued in use through to the eighteenth and nineteenth centuries. Although a number of prehistoric ovens have been excavated over the years, they are typically rare finds. Small clay ovens were found next to Neolithic hearths in Orkney at Rinyo, for example, and also at the Links of Notland. Within one Iron Age house at the hill fort site of Maiden Castle, three clay ovens were found together and would have presumably been used by the community as a whole—if indeed their intended use was the baking of bread. The relative scarcity of ovens during the prehistoric period suggests that they might have had a very different use. Malt drying is certainly one plausible suggestion that has been put forward. Malt was an important addition to the diet and required the slow toasting of soaked and swollen cereal grains, either for later baking and cooking, or for the brewing of beer. Without some kind of dedicated drying oven, one is forced to toast the grains in a clay pot beside the fire that has to be constantly rotated.

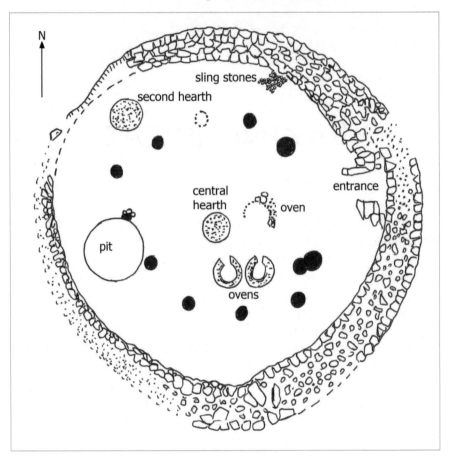

This Iron Age roundhouse at Maiden Castle hill fort in Dorset is remarkable for the number of ovens found within it. Were they used for baking bread, for drying corn, or for preparing malt ready for the process of brewing beer? (*J. Renfrew*)

Grinding

Before the dough comes anywhere near the fire, the flour has to be liberated from the grains. Ancient strains of wheat like emmer and spelt taste very similar to modern bread types, although their grains are much larger. This might seem counter intuitive in an industry that strives to cultivate ever larger fruits and vegetables, but the reasons are sound. Modern, smaller grains ripen more quickly in the fields, which reduces the time (and cost) of drying in granaries. Additionally, they shed their husks easily and uniformly, allowing for fast and efficient processing. Ancient emmer grains, however, are not only much larger, but must be heated to separate the husks from their grains. This means that any delay in harvesting a modern wheat can be catastrophic, since the farmer faces the prospect of the grains ripening in the fields. In prehistory these bigger and more stubborn wheat strains did not over-ripen if left to stand in the field.

Once threshed and winnowed and with the grains completely separated from their husks, the grains were put into sacks, storage jars, or grain pits. Wheat grains have their own tough outer jackets that protect the flour within; only on the day the flour was needed was it liberated from the grain through grinding. This was the 'daily grind', probably carried out by the women of the roundhouse family. Throughout the Neolithic and Bronze Age the type of grindstone used was called the saddle quern, made up of a lightly dished, roughly oval lower stone and a smaller hand stone. Grains are scattered onto the lower stone and then ground using the upper hand stone by pushing backwards and forwards. The most comfortable way to do this is while kneeling over the quern, and many female Neolithic skeletons display osteoarthritis in the toes, knees or lower back as a result of this daily drudge.

During the Iron Age the rotary quern was introduced into Britain. This new design consisted of a stationary lower stone and a circular upper stone. The upper stone was pierced by a central hole and was rotated around a spindle that passed through it. Grain was dropped into the hole to be caught between the two rotating stones. To move the upper stone, a single hole was cut into its side and a wooden handle inserted. It is likely that the handle was used to rotate the grindstone through 90 degrees or less, rather than in a complete circle. Certainly our own work with rotary querns suggests that this to and fro motion is the more ergonomically efficient method of grinding.

There were various regional variations of the Iron Age rotary quern, among them the beehive quern, which was popular throughout northern England. These quern stones featured conical, or bun-shaped, upper stones. Querns of the later Iron Age and Roman period were more saucer shaped in design. It is essential when using a quern to place a woven mat or sheet of leather beneath it in order to catch the flour that spills out from between the stones. Some of this will be mixed with unground cereal grains and will require regrinding. It must have been common practice to scoop enough wheat grains from a storage bin to provide wheat for the whole family for one day. With the grains in a basket by the quern, the family member tasked with grinding the day's bread would know exactly how much had to be ground and she would stop when the basket was empty.

Baking

We are lucky to have fragments of carbonized loaves from Iron Age Glastonbury to study. After analysis the loaves were found to contain fragments of wheat, hulled barley, wild oat, chess (brome grass), and a seed of common orache. It seems the loaves were unleavened, in fact the 'bread' had probably been made up as a stiff porridge, rolled into balls, flattened and then baked. The presence of wild oats and orache seeds indicate that 'weeds' must have grown within the Glastonbury wheat fields and were harvested incidentally, rather than as a crop in their own right. Archaeologists in Sweden have uncovered Viking flatbreads within cremation burials that also included a variety of mixed cereals, from flax seeds to barley, bean flour to wild oats. Multigrain flatbreads like this may have been the product of sloppy weeding, but we must remember that there were no gourmet chefs in the Bronze Age or Iron Age, and no Mrs Beeton, either, to whom roundhouse cooks could turn. Families survived on what they could grow. Although recipes were probably planned in advance, using ingredients planted many months previously, the multigrain flat bread must have been eaten when supplies were meagre and 'any and all' cereals were fed into the quern.

How is bread baked without an oven? The answer to that is: 'any way you can'. We have already seen how ash cake is baked directly in the embers of the hearth, with ash from the fire piled on top. Dough could also be placed on to a flat stone next to the fire, and as the fire heated the stone, the bread was baked. Both Scandinavia and Britain share a bakestone tradition, since their cold and damp climates favour crops like barley and oats, cereals that lend themselves well to unleavened baking. Many surviving recipes combine two or more cereal grains due to the ancient practice of sowing multiple crop types at a time.

Although leavened bread was known to the Gauls, much of what was eaten in the Celtic world was unleavened flatbread. This baked quickly and easily on hot stones, unlike leavened bread, which required a steady heat from all sides. Perhaps the limited number of Iron Age bread ovens were dedicated to baking these leavened loaves. More likely, those communities using leaven in their bread would have resorted to pot baking, where the dough is placed on a ceramic plate in the embers of the hearth, with a pot inverted to cover it. Ashes and embers were then piled on top of the pot, which heated the ceramic and then baked the bread.

Leaven

Before yeast was identified by Louis Pasteur as a living organism and the agent in fermentation, the ancient method of raising dough involved the use of leaven. Leaven is a little piece of dough saved from the last baking session that is then added to the next batch. This reserve is known as a starter or a sourdough. Essentially, the leaven is a nursery for yeast and if kept topped up with lumps of newly made dough, can survive for months, years, and even decades. Canadian trappers and gold-seekers all cultivated their own sourdoughs, and it was said that these starters were handed down through the generations. The Roman writer Pliny recorded the use of leaven in Rome:

> The leaven is prepared from the meal that is used for making the bread. For this purpose, some of the meal is kneaded before adding the salt, and is then boiled to the consistency of porridge, and left till it begins to turn sour. In most cases, however, they do not warm it at all, but only make use of a little of the dough that has been kept from the day before.

Pliny, *Natural History*, 18.26

Mix a small amount of spelt flour with warm water and mix to create a rather wet dough. This must be formed into a ball and a deep indentation made in its centre. Before pouring a little warm water into this hollow, the top of the dough is scored crossways with a knife. Set aside at room temperature for a few days, but check on the leaven regularly. Add a little flour or warm water as needed to maintain the same consistency. It should be developing a 'yeasty' or sour aroma. Soon the leaven will swell and split, which indicates that fermentation has taken place and that it is ready to be used as a source of yeast when making bread dough. Keep it inside a small clay jar and cover with a piece of cloth tied around at the top. Leaven will be susceptible to cold or frost and in prehistory must have been kept warm near the fire or (like those hardy Canadian pioneers) taken to bed.

To use the leaven, pull away three-quarters of the dough and drop into the mixing bowl before making up a fresh batch of bread dough. Remember to replace what has been taken with fresh flour and water. A healthy starter must be used once a week, with the missing dough replaced with more flour and water. This allows the yeast to flourish. In the roundhouse, this would not have been a problem, since bread-making was a daily occurrence.

Beaker Bread

This is leavened pot bread, baked in the embers. We call it Beaker Bread after the most famous and elegant of prehistoric pottery, the Bronze Age Beaker, although those cups were used only for drinking and certainly not for baking!

- 500 g spelt or emmer flour
- 15 g leaven
- 1 tsp Sea salt
- About 250 ml milk and water mixed

The dough will stick like glue to the inner surface of the two pots unless they have first been sealed. Either smear the inside of the pots with butter, or temper them with a coat of hemp or flax oil and heat in the embers. Do this two or three times to fully treat the earthenware. Next make up a dough with the flour, salt, water, milk, and leaven (use modern dried yeast if replicating this recipe). This is prehistoric cookery and the amounts are only guides, so add only a little water at a time to the mixture. Leave to rise in a warm place for half an hour and then knead thoroughly. Leave the dough to stand once more, this time for around an hour. Divide the dough up, with each portion allotted to a separate earthenware plate. Next, place a large ceramic cook pot over each plate and stand near the fire for another thirty minutes. You can then place the pots carefully onto a bed of embers. Pile ashes and embers onto the sides and top of the pots as you are able. Bake this way in the hearth for at least forty-five minutes, though be ready to put the pots back into the fire should the bread turn out to be under baked.

Dobunni Bread

You might notice some similarity between the Glastonbury flatbread, mentioned earlier, to *ugali*, the porridge-like cereal food cooked today in East Africa. Whereas *ugali* is eaten straight from the pan, however, the Iron Age bread that was discovered intact at the Glastonbury lake village was cooked into a porridge and then baked on a hot stone. In this it was very similar to Yorkshire riddle bread, which is traditionally cooked as a porridge and left overnight before baking on a hot bakestone.

Dobunni bread is my own version of the flat bread that was eaten on the Somerset Levels and is named after the powerful Celtic tribe that lived nearby, the Dobunni. It smells and tastes a little like a Staffordshire oatcake.

- 200 g spelt wheat flour
- 200 g barley meal
- 100 g oatmeal
- 25 g ground flax or poppy seed
- 1 tsp Sea salt
- About 250 ml water

Over the fire, make up a thick porridge with the wheat flour, barley meal, and oats. Grind up the flax seeds and add them to the pot. When ready, spoon the mixture onto a plate and then leave it overnight in a warm place. Next day, add a little salt to the dish and then drop spoonfuls of the mixture onto a hot stone that is sat across the hearth. Pat these down so that each flat bread is as thin as it can possibly be without falling apart. Bake each side of the Dobunni bread for ten minutes (although this will vary depending on the temperature of the embers and the thickness of the bakestone—always check the bread before removing it from the stone).

Celtic Flatbread

Simply flour and water, this is a basic prehistoric flatbread.

- 250 g spelt flour
- 1 tsp sea salt
- About 150 ml water

Mix the flour, water, and salt into a dough and knead well. Next, roll the dough into a thick sausage and divide up into half a dozen equal portions. Roll each of these out as thinly as the dough will allow. It may seem natural to roll out the flatbreads as perfect circles, but the shape required is determined by your bakestone. If rectangular, then your flatbread needs to be something resembling that shape in order to fit.

Lay the flatbread onto a hot stone by the fire and bake it there on both sides for three to four minutes. Take care not to burn the bread and check frequently.

Haverbread

Haverbread is a traditional Yorkshire oatcake, baked on a hot stone or griddle over the fire. The term haverbread may come from the Norse word *hafrecreed* ('oat porridge') and the word, at least, probably arrived in Britain with the Norsemen who colonized much of the north.

- 150 g oatmeal
- 1 tsp sea salt
- 2 tsp melted bacon fat or lard
- About 100 ml water

Mix the oatmeal, salt, and water together, then pour in the melted bacon fat or lard. If it is inconvenient to melt the fat, then mash it up with a spoon or a knife (there were no forks in British prehistory). Stir well and continue to add water until a stiff paste is formed. Break the mixture in two and on a flat surface (dusted with oatmeal) roll both into balls, then roll these out until they are around half a centimetre thick. Check that your two haverbreads will fit onto your bakestone and then bake for around three to four minutes until they are nicely browned. Turn them halfway through the baking process.

Blaanda Bread

This is another recipe with Norse connections, this time originating from the Shetland Islands. Blaanda bread is very similar to Dobunni bread, but instead of using water it is instead made with full fat milk. Add a drizzle of honey and a knob of butter to the mixture and elevate this bread from farming staple to chieftain's treat.

Beer Bread

Alcohol and bread have a close and ancient relationship, since the fermentation of barley or wheat is central to both processes. There must have been a degree of overlap, where the yeast in one process helped to kick start the fermentation in another. The ancient writer Pliny remarks that:

> In Gaul and Spain, where they make a drink by steeping [grain] ... they employ the foam which thickens upon the surface as a leaven, hence it is that the bread in those countries is lighter than that made elsewhere.

> Pliny, *Natural History*, 18.12

People of Gaul, which in Pliny's day was under Roman rule, may have eaten Roman-style bread. His comment should certainly not be taken to suggest that all Gauls, or indeed all Celtic peoples, regularly ate leavened bread.

- 250 ml beer dregs (brown ale is best)
- 400 g spelt flour
- 1 tsp sea salt
- 2 tsp honey

Leave the beer uncovered for a day or so before using in this recipe. When ready to bake, mix the flour with the beer. Knead gently then put aside in a warm place for two hours. Later, add the salt and honey, kneading thoroughly once again. Add more water or flour as needed to maintain the correct consistency. Bake the bread just like Beaker Bread, described above.

Celtic Bean Cakes

Not exactly bread, these flat bean cakes are baked on a hot stone, just like haver cakes or flatbread.

- 60 g butter
- 250 g processed Celtic beans
- 1 small cup of chopped hazelnuts
- Bunch of chopped chives
- 1 tsp sea salt
- 1 egg
- A little flour

The beans, if dried, should be soaked overnight and then drained. Cook the beans until tender, drain the water and add the hazelnuts as well as the chopped chives and sea salt. Beat the egg and then add that, too. Mix well, adding a little flour as needed to create a nice, stiff mixture that is not too sloppy and wet. Once the right consistency is reached, shape portions into small flat cakes and place on a hot bakestone. Turn midway through cooking.

Malted Bread

The process of malting involves soaking wheat or barley grains until they sprout, then baking them, and grinding the dried sprouts into malt. Malt gives this bread its own distinctive flavour.

- 500 g spelt flour
- 1 cup of wheat malt
- 1 tsp sea salt
- About 250 ml water

Add the malt and sea salt to the flour then begin mixing, all the time adding water until the right consistency is reached—neither too sticky nor too dry. Knead well and then break into fist-sized balls that you can roll out until they are perhaps a half-centimetre thick. Bake these on a hot stone for ten minutes each side, but check the bread frequently.

Flax Bread

- 200 g spelt wheat
- 50 g flax meal
- 1 tsp sea salt
- About 100 ml water

Follow the instructions for baking Malted Bread (above), but substitute the cup of wheat malt for a small amount of flax meal.

Autumn Bread

This is a sweet bread than can be baked in the late summer or autumn.

- 500 g spelt flour
- 1 large cup of blackberries
- Half cup of chopped hazelnuts
- 200 g honey
- About 250 ml water

Mix the flour with the salt, hazelnuts, and blackberries; add water little by little, stirring continuously in order to make a dough that is not too dry or wet. Add the honey at this stage. The blackberries bring with them a lot of juice and care must be taken not to let the mixture get too sloppy; if it is, then add a little more flour. Once a satisfactory dough has been produced, it should be broken up into small cakes, rolled out and placed onto a hot bakestone. Depending on the temperature of the stone and the thickness of the flatbreads, they should be ready in ten to twenty minutes. Check the underside for scorching, and turn the bread halfway through baking.

10

THE CLAY POT

Pottery is an invention that accompanied agriculture and the domestication of animals. Although there is no technical reason why the hunter-gatherers of Star Carr could not take river clay and fabricate cooking pots of their own, the mobile lifestyle of the Mesolithic tribes was at odds with the heavy, fragile nature of the earthenware containers.

Archaeologists have imagined hunters cooking their meat on wooden spits, or over the embers of their camp fires. They have also suggested that meat could be cooked in leather bags hung over the fire, an idea that may sound farfetched, but certainly has parallels in human history. The Greek writer and historian Herodotus recorded the habits of the Scythian nomads, living in southern Russia around 450 BC:

> As Scythia is utterly barren of firewood, a plan was contrived for boiling the flesh, which is the following: after flaying the beasts, they take out all the bones, and (if they possess such gear) put the flesh into cauldrons. If they do not happen to possess a cauldron, they make the animals' stomachs hold the flesh and pouring in a little water, lay the bones under and light them. The bones burn beautifully; and the stomach easily contains all the flesh when it is stripped from the bones, so that by this plan your ox is made to boil himself...

> Herodotus, *Histories*, 4.61

Settled family life in the Neolithic focussed around the hearth and here the clay cook pot came into its own. Now a number of ingredients could be combined and cooked together to form stews, soups and broths reliably and conveniently. From beef bourguignon to Lancashire hotpot, Chinese egg drop soup to Irish stew, the legacy of the clay cooking pot remains with us today.

Pottery Types

Pottery for much of prehistory served as a method of cooking and for the storage of foods and liquids. The earliest pots of the Neolithic were plain and round-bottomed in shape, but over time impressed decoration began to appear on these bowls. For much of the period two styles dominated— Peterborough ware, with its thick, coarse clay walls, heavy rims, and lots of impressed decoration, and grooved ware, which adopted a simple bucket shape with grooved ornamentation running in geometric patterns. Although Peterborough ware is often found at burial sites, grooved ware is always found within domestic contexts and because of this we can be sure that it served as a Neolithic cookpot or storage jar. Beakers arrived in Britain at the start of the Early Bronze Age and these fine, handsomely decorated drinking vessels may have been used for drinking mead or beer.

Fashions in cook pot design continued to evolve in the Bronze Age with so-called food vessels, which featured heavy bevelled rims, and with the cinerary urns, of which the collared urns were the most widespread. Small decorated pots often labelled as incense or 'pygmy' jars were also used in the Bronze Age and Jane Renfrew believes these little jars might have held salt, the trade in which developed at around this time. They might just as easily have held butter, edible plant seeds or leaven. With metal now available, some of

Grooved ware pottery from the Neolithic period. (*J. Thomas*)

the wealthiest families could boast cauldrons made of sheet bronze, carefully riveted together. Cauldrons continued to be made in the Iron Age and were complimented with iron firedogs and even iron and bronze bowls. Yet pottery continued to be used by the masses and during the early Iron Age these designs seem to have been imitations of those found on the continent. Through time a variety of different regional styles began to develop; in the south of Britain the vertical-sided saucepan ware pots were popular. Even these displayed great variety in profile and decoration from one site to another. By the start of the first century BC the potter's wheel appeared in Britain, bringing some uniformity to the pottery styles of the Late Iron Age. Handmade pottery did not disappear altogether, though, as finds of Glastonbury Ware in the south west indicate.

Early Iron Pottery

Cook pots were designed for the fire with flat bottoms, deep bodies, and thick walls. The clay was typically mixed with 'grog', which may have been sand, crushed shell, chopped straw, or ground-up pottery. This helped the pot to withstand the thermal shock of differential heating and prevented shrinkage when the newly made pot was drying. Cook pots were communal, and when the food within was ready it was ladled out into individual bowls. Most likely every family member had their own wooden or pottery bowl and spoon (either of wood or horn). During the Late Iron Age, an era of very conspicuous consumption, some of the pottery serving bowls were polished and finely made—they were statements of wealth as much as pieces of crockery. Contact with Roman culture brought access to olive oil, wine, and other luxuries, new ways to show off at feast-time.

Cooking with a Clay Pot

If there is one piece of clay pot advice to impart to a beginner, it is: be gentle. We are used to throwing a saucepan onto the stove, turning the heat up full blast, and cooking. The clay pot, no matter how thick-walled and sturdy in appearance, must be warmed slowly. It is the differential heating of the fabric, hot in one area, cold in another, which will cause the pot to crack—with fatal results. While the fire is still in its infancy, the prudent act is place the cook pot (holding a little water) on the edge of the hearth. As the fire builds, the pot can be turned at infrequent intervals in order to warm it through.

When the time comes to bring the pot together with direct heat, it is best to avoid flame. A bed of embers, however, is ideal and the flat-based design of most prehistoric cooking vessels suggests that roundhouse cooks were of the same mind. Adding water to the pot as it warms allows for a little heat transference away from the vulnerable walls of the vessel; I never place empty pottery onto the hearth. If the coals begin to cool, the correct procedure is the quick removal of the pot using a handy pot cloth (the prehistoric equivalent of the oven glove), followed by the shovelling of new coals into position. Finally, the pot is carefully lowered back onto the embers. When cooking begins, the warm water within the pot can be poured away and then immediately replaced with meat or vegetables (as the recipe demands). Stews and soups require water or stock to be added in some quantity, this must be added very slowly, a little bit at a time, to prevent the vessel walls from cracking. Always be aware of the risk to the pot. If a thick stew or pottage is desired, then go easy on the water you are adding. It is easy to add more but difficult to take it back out. Once all of the stock or water is in the pot, the stew can be left to simmer gently. If the food is bubbling furiously, then the heat is far too high and after the pot is temporarily removed, some of the embers can be pushed away, back into the fire. Simmering will take anything from one to two hours, depending on the size of the pot and the temperature of the embers. The fire must be tended and the heat regulated carefully and the pot might also benefit from being turned occasionally.

Other than breaking the pot in the fire, the greatest danger lies in overcooking the food. There is no 'Gas Mark 6' or '180 degrees' setting on the hearth and so cooking heat is dependent on eye, on taste, and on experience. Making things doubly difficult is the narrow neck on some prehistoric pots, making it tough to get a good look at the state of the food within. What colour is the meat? Is the stock bubbling? Are those greens limp yet? Some designs, like the Neolithic grooved ware, are relatively wide-mouthed, which nullifies this problem. Still, the roundhouse environment is a dark one, and in such conditions it can be difficult to observe how the food cooks within even straight sided-pots like the grooved ware. These two mysterious variables, the temperature and state of the food, often drive experimental cooks to sit it out and the end result will invariably be an unappetising grey mush. I recommend small samples of the stew be regularly spooned into a bowl for analysis. Check out the meat and the vegetables—take the bowl outside into the sunlight if need be.

When the pot is removed from the fire, either temporarily in order to manage the coal bed, or at the end of cooking, I place it on a piece of flat timber. This absorbs the heat of the earthenware, preventing it from scorching the ground, it will not chip the pot and provides a known, reliable place in the roundhouse environment for the placement of a hot pot. From there the finished stew, soup, or pottage can be ladled out into individual eating bowls. Always serve with bread as it was in prehistory. It should be noted that earthenware vessels absorb some of the flavours from each delicious meal that has gone before, since the fat penetrates deep into the clay fabric. The Roman writer and gourmet Apicius recommended that a new cook pot be employed when preparing many of dishes he describes. Fish, in particular, has the potential to permanently taint a food vessel. I clean the clay pots that I use as soon as they have cooled down of their own accord—the dangers of trying to wash or rinse out a pot that is still warm are obvious. Remember, also, to dry the pot thoroughly; a wet earthenware jar left for too long in a cool place will only attract mould, which will soon spread across the whole jar, inside and out.

Clay Pot Recipes

Springtime Soup
In April or May, a delicious soup can be cooked from the juicy young leaves that are newly emerged from the chill of winter. You may vary the amounts and types of leaves used, but my springtime soup included leaves of dandelion, chive, ground ivy, and hawthorn. Hawthorn leaves are only palatable during the spring—do not pick them in late summer. I added yellow gorse flowers and both the stems, leaves, and flowers of red deadnettle. Both added a dash of colour to the dish. Fry the greens in butter and then add water gradually until the correct consistency is reached for soup. Simmer gently for twenty minutes.

Frumenty
Frumenty is possibly one of the oldest meals known to the prehistoric farmers of Britain and is made up simply of wheat grains soaked in water, which are then cooked in a pot. First, the grains are washed and then put into a clay pot with water to cover them. The pot sits by the fire for twelve hours, and must be turned regularly. During this time, the wheat grains should swell and then burst, and the stewed or 'creed' wheat should resemble a thick porridge. At the end of this time, if the wheat has not creed, then try boiling the mixture for five minutes or so. Frumenty has been served up in a variety of ways over the centuries, but for the poor farming family will have been eaten as it was, spooned out of the pot, perhaps with a pinch of salt. Honey, ground hazelnuts, or fresh berries do make a nice addition to frumenty.

Pease Pudding
Like frumenty, pease pudding was a simple and very basic recipe. It was a way to easily turn a dried and stored crop into a substantial meal.

- 250 g dried peas
- Sprig of mint
- 25 g butter
- Sea salt
- One egg (optional)

Dried peas are taken from storage and soaked in water overnight to soften them. Once drained, the peas are cooked in fresh water with a few mint leaves. Drain them once again and then mash; add a pinch of salt and one beaten egg (if desired). Now the pea mixture is tied into a floured cloth and hung to cook in a cauldron or large cookpot. The pease pudding will absorb flavours from the meat stock that is cooking in the pot. Simmer gently for an hour and then serve with the meat.

Marrow Bones

The marrow bones should come from the centre of a round of beef or from any part of the legs. The open ends of the bones must first be covered with a simple paste of flour and water to prevent the marrow oozing from the bone during cooking. Water is then brought to the boil in a pot and the marrow bones are placed upright in the water. After approximately twenty minutes the bones are removed and the marrow teased out with a knife. The marrow is soft and best served spread onto bread.

Venison Stew

Red deer and roe deer were hunted throughout prehistory, even after Britons settled down to farm the land. A study of prehistoric bone remains in Buckinghamshire indicated that hunted animals (mainly red and roe deer) made up around 5 per cent or less of the total.

- 500 g venison, cubed
- 250 ml of vegetable or meat stock
- 100 g of chopped pig nut (or parsnip)
- 1 tsp sea salt
- One bunch of chopped chives
- 25 g butter

Fry the venison in butter until brown, then add the pig nut (or chopped parsnip if pig nut is unavailable) and the chives. Add salt and then pour in the vegetable stock. I used what left-over stock I had from a batch of springtime soup. Allow the stew to simmer for an hour before serving with bread.

Soay Stew

Mutton refers to meat from sheep that is over two years old (lamb meat, on the other hand, is generally from an animal that has been reared for only five months). Some farmers argue that mutton should be the meat from a wether (a castrated male sheep), since it is believed that castration improves the taste. William Kitchiner in *The Cook's Oracle*, from 1817, declared that the finest mutton came from a five-year-old wether.

- 500 g lamb or mutton
- 4 whole ramson bulbs
- 12 juniper berries
- 1 tsp sea salt
- 1 tsp spelt flour
- One bunch of chives
- 50 g pearl barley
- 25 g butter

The lamb is diced and then dusted with flour. Next it is fried in butter inside a warmed pot until brown. Add the juniper berries and salt along with the chopped ramson bulbs (or alternatively use a small leek). Cook for a few minutes and then add the grains of pearl barley with enough water to cover the ingredients. Keep the pot simmering gently over a bed of coals for at least two hours, but keep an eye on the stew—add more water if the stew looks like it is drying out.

Wild Boar Stew

The combination of pork, apple, and beer produces a delicious dish that simply tastes 'right'. One might think beer is wasted in cooking meat, but it produces a wonderful stock. Wheat beer is specified here as it is mentioned as the drink of the Gauls by the ancient writer Athenaeus.

- 500 g wild boar or pork loin
- 4 crab apples
- 100 g peas
- 1 tsp sea salt
- One bunch of chives
- 25 g butter
- 500 ml wheat beer

To cook the wild boar stew you must first soak the peas overnight (if they are dried). Chop the pork and fry in butter within a clay pot that has been warmed by the fire. Add the chopped chives and wheat beer, then top up with enough water to cover the ingredients. Drop in the salt and simmer for around an hour, after which time the chopped apple can be added. Simmer for another hour or so over embers.

Smokey Fish Stew

- 200 g bacon
- 4 whole ramson bulbs
- 250 g of smoked fish
- 1 tsp sea salt
- 1 litre full fat milk
- One bunch of chives
- Several dandelion leaves
- 25 g lard

Smoking food helped to preserve it and this recipe uses two smoked ingredients, fish and bacon. Most of the meals eaten by a prehistoric household will have included dried foods (peas, Celtic beans, pearl barley, etc.) or smoked meats. The bacon is fried in the lard; do not use modern, finely cut streaky bacon, but thicker, knife-cut bacon or gammon. Add the chopped chives and dandelion leaves, then add the chopped fillets of smoked fish. Milk is used to cover the ingredients and can be topped up with a little water if needed. Gently simmer the smoky fish stew for around an hour over a bed of coals, stirring regularly.

Beef and Beer Stew

The Celtic palate appreciated both beef and beer in equal measure. The ancient author Posidonios, quoted by Athenaeus, tells us that: 'Their food consists of a few loaves of bread, but of large quantities of meat prepared in water or roasted over coals or on spits' (Athenaeus 4.151). Cattle bones are a common find in domestic middens, which attests to their love of beef. When Julius Caesar defeated the British defenders of Bigbury hill, near Canterbury, for example, his troops discovered a large herd of cattle that had been corralled there.

- 500 g beef steak
- 150 g field mushrooms
- 25 g butter
- 1 tsp sea salt
- tsp of juniper berries
- 1 tsp spelt flour
- 500 ml of beer (use brown ale)
- 1 bunch of greens (sea beet, fat hen or garlic mustard)
- 50 g honey

The beef is cut into cubes and, after dusting with flour, is lightly fried in butter inside a pot that has been warmed by the fire. Add mushrooms to the pot along with the pinch of salt and a splash of water. Once the mushrooms begin to change colour you can add the juniper berries, greens, and cover the mixture with beer—top up with water if required. The stew is then set to simmer for a couple of hours over hot embers. The writer and researcher Jacqui Wood puts honey into her beef and beer stew; I agree that this addition provides a wonderfully flavourful contrast.

Black Pudding

Despite the lack of hard evidence, it is quite likely that cattle were bled during the winter months. Most of the herd will have been kept in a byre, close to the roundhouse, and so frequent access to the cattle will have been easy. The process provided food that, just like milking, did not mean sacrificing one of the herd. While the Masaai of East Africa mix the blood of their cattle with milk and drink the result, the roundhouse cook will probably have made black pudding instead, a dish that was certainly eaten by the Greeks around 800 BC.

> And as when a man before a great blazing fire turns swiftly this way and that a paunch full of fat and blood, and is very eager to have it roasted quickly, so Odysseus tossed from side to side.

> Homer, *Odyssey*, 20

Historically, crofters from Stornoway (on the island of Lewis) made black puddings from sheep that had been slaughtered and then hung in order to collect the animal's blood. Next the intestines were removed and washed thoroughly in brine. After being turned inside out they were left to soak for a full day. The skins were then rinsed first in cold, and then hot, water, which softened the surfaces and allowed the crofters to then scrape them clean. Oatmeal, or some other cereal, would have been added to the blood along with a cup of flour and some fat from the animal (on Lewis they still use beef suet, which is fat taken from around the kidneys). Heated and mixed to form a porridge-like consistency, the mixture was then fed into the skins. Once prepared, the individual black puddings were left for up to three days before boiling in water for an hour. Some Scottish households stored their black puddings in barrels of oatmeal, in order to keep them cool.

In the roundhouse, black pudding would have been sliced and then either baked on a hot stone next to the fire, or added to a pot of stew.

Celtic Bean and Pork

- 250 g bacon or gammon
- 200 g Celtic beans
- 80 g pignut root
- Bunch of ramson leaves
- 1 tsp sea salt
- Butter

Pork and beans have been eaten together for centuries and make a filling and tasty dish. The roundhouse cook would have taken dried Celtic beans from her food store and soaked them overnight. Once the fire is lit the bacon is chopped and then fried in butter within a warmed clay pot. If Celtic or 'tic' beans are unavailable then use the modern broad bean, which makes a reasonable substitute. Today tic beans are grown mainly as animal feed, since they require far more processing to make them palatable than other modern beans. Chopped pignut root is then added, along with the ramson leaves. Both have modern substitutes: parsnip can stand in for pignut at a pinch and a few slices of leek provide the hot onion taste that the ramson greens would have given. Add water, just enough to cover the mixture, and season with a sprinkle of sea salt.

Porridge

- 300 g oatmeal
- Pinch of sea salt
- 1 tbsp. honey
- Handful of blackberries or raspberries

The Scots will tell you that a decent porridge is made with oats, salt, and hot water, with no sugar or milk in sight. They are almost correct. Ancient porridge, such as the *pulmentum* eaten by Rome's plebs as well as its legionaries, was a thicker version of gruel that was made of spelt flour mixed with water and a sprinkle of salt, and mixed over the fire to the consistency of porridge. In Roman society, this served the same purpose as gruel, which was a much more watery affair.

Of course, any cereal grain could be used to make porridge—wheat flour, barley flour, even oatmeal. Waking up in the roundhouse, our own breakfast began with porridge, although we turned our noses up at *pulmentum* and instead decided to cook oatmeal porridge in water. When it was ready to be served up to the bleary-eyed diners, I added a drop of honey to each bowl and a few blackberries. Cooking with milk, despite the added benefits of calcium and energy-giving fats, smacked of luxury. Nevertheless, the oatmeal and summer fruits porridge was delicious. It was made more so being eaten from wooden bowls around a rekindled fire, with shafts of summer sunrise slicing diagonally into the dim interior of the roundhouse.

Warm up a little water in the pot by the fire. When it begins to boil, add the oatmeal and stir. Continue stirring, while adding more and more water—all the while maintaining a porridge-like consistency in the mixture. As it stiffens, add a touch more water. Never leave the pot over the embers, else the porridge will dry quickly and burn on to the bottom and sides of your clay pot—this is a dish that cannot be left to its own devices. When ready (give it fifteen minutes), serve with a dribble of honey and a few berries.

Oats with Nettle and Pork

- 300 g oatmeal
- 250 g nettle leaves
- One bunch of chives
- 1 tsp sea salt
- 25 g lard
- 150 g pork

Nettles seem an unlikely food source, but the leaves, once boiled, are perfectly edible. In fact the plant as a whole is incredibly valuable. I have attended several flint-knapping courses over the years and perhaps the most useful skill I learnt was to make fibre (string) from the stems of nettle.

The basics are easy to describe. We first snapped a nettle stem off at the base and, upending it, used our bare hand to strip off the leaves (which sting only on their upper surfaces). Next the stems were gently crushed with a stone so that the long fibres within the stem were exposed. These were then picked out from the woody outer layers and laid to dry. Later we took three of the dried inner fibres at a time and twisted them together in a method that is simple to do, but very difficult to describe. As we reached the ends of the fibres, it was time to pick up three more and introduce those to the twisting process, in this way a continuous length of nettle fibre could be made. As we perfected our skills, the tutor revealed a coil of rope that he had been working on for several weeks. It had required many phases of fibre twisting, eventually feeding thicker and thicker lengths of the nettle thread together to create the rope. Rope like that, I pondered, probably hoisted the great sarsen stones that formed the latest and grandest stage of Stonehenge.

Whatever use the ropes and cord were put to, whether it was tying up beams during the construction of the roundhouse, creating a binding to haft an axe or flint blade on to its handle, weaving a fishing net or creating a simple belt, the process would have created a lot of nettle leaves—and these could be eaten. Doubtless, then, this summer activity must have been accompanied by various nettle-based dishes. Oats with nettle and pork is presented in that spirit.

Fry the pieces of chopped pork in lard within a clay pot, which has been warmed by the fire. When browning nicely, add the oatmeal and just enough water to cover it. As it cooks, check frequently that the mixture does not dry out and do not hesitate to add extra water if needed. Once the oatmeal begins to swell, add both the chopped chives and nettles. Next, add the salt. Simmer the mixture for around an hour, but be careful that it does not dry out and always be ready to add a little water if required. The nutritious nettle greens are put to good use in a filling dish (the oatmeal sees to that) that is tasty and appetising (the bacon sees to that). It certainly beats eating nettle leaves that have simply been boiled in water.

Gruel

Prehistoric communities probably relied on gruel, perhaps serving it up at least once a day. Societies throughout history have eaten this basic dish; after all, it is simply flour boiled in plenty of water or milk. If there was neither meat nor vegetables to be had, then there was always barley or wheat flour, which could be added to water and boiled in a clay pot over the fire. It was a subsistence food that tapped into the staple food source of the prehistoric— cereal grain. Gruel, along with frumenty and unleavened bread, formed the true taste of British prehistory. Talk of pork loins, spit roasted goose, and beef in beer stews hides the fact that these were luxury foods, meals for feasts and high days and for days of plenty. Day in and day out, gruel, frumenty, and flat breads dominated the serving bowls of the poorest farmers, particularly in winter when fresh vegetables, fruits, and foraged greens were in desperately short supply.

Evidence of gruel in the diet of Iron Age folk comes from the remarkably well-preserved bodies that have been found in bogs across northern Europe. The anaerobic environment of these peat bogs prevented decay and effectively stopped time for these unfortunate Iron Age victims—nearly all seem to have been murdered. Archaeologists have been able to study with great intimacy their final hours; Tollund Man, for example, had been drinking water rich in sphagnum moss and his last meal was cooked over a fire of burning heather wood. Of interest to us are the contents of Tollund Man's stomach—his last meal. It seems he ate gruel, a dish containing neither meat nor green vegetables. All of the ingredients (and there were forty different kinds) were seeds or grains, many of which were from low-yield grass cereals, hard to harvest runt-grains, and plants that we now recognize as weeds. There was plenty of chaff in evidence as well as a little grit or sand within the gruel, too. What kind of a meal was this? Immediately we can say that this was not part of a normal diet; chaff and dirt, essentially the scrapings from a roundhouse threshing floor, were obviously not on the typical Celtic menu. Perhaps it would help us to explore the nature of these deaths and the status of these victims. Almost universally, the bodies had been murdered—some had their throats cut (Grauballe Man), some were hanged or strangled to death (Huldremose Woman and Tollund Man), and there were others who had their heads smashed in (Clonycavan Man). Some unfortunates, like Lindow Man, had been stabbed, strangled, and beaten to death.

The Roman writer Tacitus, in his treatise on the German tribes, tells us about executions in the northern bogs:

> Penalties are distinguished according to the offence. Traitors and deserters are hanged on trees; the coward, the unwarlike, the man stained with abominable vices, is plunged into the mire of the morass, with a hurdle put over him. This distinction in punishment means that crime, they think, ought, in being punished, to be exposed, while infamy ought to be buried out of sight.

> Tacitus, *Germania* 12

Tacitus later describes the religious rites associated with the Germanic goddess Nerthus. A statue of her was paraded throughout the region and venerated by all who saw it. When the goddess on her cart is returned to the sacred lake from which she came, the cart, the holy symbols, and the goddess herself, are washed.

> This service is performed by slaves, says Tacitus, who are immediately afterwards drowned in the lake. Thus mystery begets terror and pious reluctance to ask what the sight can be that only those doomed to die may see.

> Tacitus, *Germania* 40

Julius Caesar likewise reported the practice of human sacrifice amongst the Celtic tribes of Gaul:

> The Gauls believe the power of the gods can only be appeased if one human life is exchanged for another and they have sacrifices of this kind regularly established by the community.... They believe that the gods prefer it if the people executed have been caught in the act of theft or armed robbery or some other crime, but when the supply of victims runs out, they even go to the extent of sacrificing innocent men.

> Julius Caesar, *Gallic War*, 6.16

Either the bog bodies are criminals who have been formally executed by the community, or they are human sacrifices to one of the Celtic or Germanic gods. The violence inflicted on some of the bog victims, and the way in which a number were bound or staked to the ground, certainly favours the former, while the neatly trimmed nails of Lindow Man and the care with which some bodies were placed into the bog, favours the latter. Perhaps it is immaterial. Tollund Man had eaten gruel before his death, as had Windeby Girl, Lindow Man, Grauballe Man, and dozens more. If they had been criminals, tied to a post for days while the tribe decided their fate, it is not unreasonable to suggest that these outcasts would be fed the roughest of food, a gruel made up of the floor sweepings, the dropped seeds and chaff, and unhusked barley grains. And if these bog victims had been ritual sacrifices, perhaps willingly, then how might we interpret such a meagre and demeaning last meal? Historically, human sacrifice was only performed during times of great crisis within a community. We might easily imagine that famine marked the most common crisis that a farming community might encounter. It might be that Tollund Man had no meat in his gut and that his last meal was an inadequate, desperately scraped together bowl of gruel because that was all his tribe could offer. Starvation and famine might have triggered the need for some of these human sacrifices and the evidence for their desperation might well be the gruel within the victim's stomachs.

11

USING HOT STONES

With the wind roaring in the tops of the trees, the four men made their way along the base of the cliff, stumbling now and then with the weight of the doe. Rain looked likely and so the hunters hurried on. Soon enough the comforting smell of wood smoke reached them through the birch wood forest. There, in a small glade beneath the naked rocks of the cliff, sat the family camp. A dozen people—men, women and children were busy there, preparing the evening fire, baking hazelnuts, and tidying up after leatherwork or flint-knapping. The light was fading and the rain would be here soon.

Many hands helped with the red deer, in skinning, jointing and processing. Still, much could be left till the morrow. Tonight there would be fresh venison to eat, along with baked hazelnut, roast pignut root and acorn cakes cooked on a fireside stone. One family had baked bread using wheat grains which had been traded from families further south who (it was said) were cultivating the new crop in organised plots.

Around 5000 BC (near the end of the Mesolithic) scenes like this must have occurred at Bouldnor Cliff, a submerged site off the north-west coast of the Isle of Wight. Here on the seabed in 1999, a Mesolithic campsite was identified when divers caught a local lobster in the act of digging up flint microliths while he excavated his burrow. Today the waters of the Solent wash between the Isle of Wight and Southampton. Back in 5000 BC there was no island and the land there was dominated by a wide river valley filled with marsh and forest, through which bands of Mesolithic hunter-gatherers roamed. As the ice sheets retreated, water levels rose and the region now known as the Solent was flooded. Before the onset of this watery cataclysm, one group of hunters had settled for a time beneath a cliff that is now submerged in 10 metres of water, just off the Isle of Wight.

Divers discovered burnt flints and pieces of charcoal at Bouldnor Cliff as well as worked timbers, hazelnut shells, and even traces of wheat DNA. The wheat was a strain not native to Britain, however, and must have been traded with people from much further south who had already begun to cultivate it. This was family life in the Mesolithic, life around the cooking fire, where food had to be prepared without that most useful of human inventions—the cookpot.

In the Middle Stone Age, food could be heated on flat stones by the camp fire or on wooden spits. Some cuts of meat might even have been cooked directly on the coals, as we have seen in Chapter 7. Venison could always be cubed and threaded onto greenwood skewers to be grilled, barbeque style, but, with a dozen people waiting to be fed, another alternative was needed. We have already seen how spit roasting can effectively cook portions, or indeed the whole carcass, of an animal, but the process is intensive. It requires that the cooks remain at the fire for several hours and that the fire is constantly fed with fuel. Hunters of the Mesolithic were obviously able to spit roast their meat, and probably did. But was there another, less labour-intensive way?

Earth Ovens

Visitors to the South Pacific today may be invited to a feast where the food is cooked underground, in a pit. In New Zealand the Maori call this pit a *hangi*, while in Fiji it is known as a *lovo* and Hawaii as an *iuau*. They are all earth ovens and function in essentially the same way. Their principle use is in baking large amounts of food efficiently for a celebration or feast where many people must be fed. While we have no direct evidence for the use of earth ovens during the British Mesolithic, it is likely the technique was employed for the cooking of large joints of meat; it consumes far less fuel than spit roasting and can be left unattended.

The principle of cooking within a *hangi* or *iuau* hinges on the use of heat that is radiating from stones. A pit is dug and lined with flat stones, and a fire is then lit within the pit. While it burns, meat is prepared for cooking and given a protective wrapping of banana leaves. After two hours or so, the embers are raked out of the pit and the wrapped meat is placed on to the layer of stones (which are now fiercely hot). In some traditions more hot stones are added on top, and above these sit a layer of leaf-wrapped vegetables. Finally, the entire contents of the pit are covered with banana leaves and then a covering of sacks, tarpaulins, or earth in order to prevent heat escaping. After several hours the cooking pit is uncovered and the meat extracted and unwrapped.

My first attempt at building an earth oven was a venture into the unknown. I planned to cook two joints of pork and protect them from the ashes with a dough case, rather than banana leaves. The entire project had to be planned carefully, how long would it take the joints to cook? Unknown. How long would it take to dig and prepare the pit? How long should the fire burn for? All unknown.

Helped by hungry colleagues, I decided to pull the joints of meat out of the ground at 2 p.m., after exactly two hours of cooking. That meant the fire in the pit would need to be scraped out to expose the hot stones at midday. Working backwards, that meant we needed the fire to burn for a good hour, starting at 11 a.m., and so digging and preparing the pit needed to have been underway by 10 a.m. There was a good deal of work to be done and it was shared out between all those present. Everyone understood that to eat the food you had to help with the oven, and this proved a great motivation. Tasks were rotated, and included taking up the turf and digging the pit, chopping firewood, and collecting large stones from elsewhere on the site. Turf was lifted and a pit dug on the bare soil, but we also lifted the turf off of an area directly adjacent to the pit—this is where we would scrape the hot ashes once the fire had burnt down. We even cut a slope from the pit up to this ash area.

By midday the fire had burned down to embers and hot white ash. We used metal farming tools and wooden boards to scrape away the ashes and expose the hot, blackened stones beneath. One of us had coated the joints in bread dough while the fire burned, but this dough was not for eating, it was there only to add a layer of protection to the meat from ash and soil.

Once the dough-encrusted pork joints had been placed into the pit and a single large, flat stone was manoeuvred on top of the meat, the soil from the pit was back-filled and the turf replaced. The ground steamed for two hours. At 2 p.m. it was time to expose the earth oven and dig up the joints of meat. Unfortunately, although I knew where the pit was, I did not know the exact location of the joints. My first attempt at spade-work sliced into one of the joints and it came out of the ground a doughy, soil-encrusted mess. I was far more careful with the second joint and lifted it out whole. Cutting it in half to create a cross section, I could see clearly the crust of the baked dough and the air gap between meat and dough—it looked a little like the pastry around a meat pie.

We all dutifully tasted the pork and to our great relief it was cooked to perfection through to the middle; it tasted wonderful. The earth oven experiment had been a great success and I realised at the time that it had been good judgement to cook two joints of pork, rather than just one. With such an investment in time and energy, it makes sense to prepare a back-up in case anything goes wrong. With a communal effort and packing lots of joints into the pits, we could envisage a clan or tribe using this method of cooking during a feast or celebration. The earth oven technique of roasting meat was certainly not something the roundhouse cook was going to carry out on a daily or weekly basis, however.

Returning to our community of hunters and gatherers camped beneath Bouldnor Cliff at the end of the Mesolithic, how would they build their earth oven? Pacific islanders use banana leaves, tarpaulins, and sacking to protect and insulate the roasting food. In my first earth oven reconstruction, I had protected the meat with bread dough. For Mesolithic tribes, using dough was not an option, even if they could get their hands on imported wheat. They certainly had no banana leaves, although some native British plants such as dock might serve as a practical alternative if the leaves are of sufficient size. As for turf, without grazing animals and pasture land to create it, there was little around during the Mesolithic. Even digging out the pit and manipulating the hot stones had required iron tools that were unavailable during this period.

Those hunters carrying the red deer into camp will have excavated their cooking pit with digging sticks, the improvised tools used by some gatherer cultures today. They are discussed in Chapter 5. A length of wood, roughly wrist-thick, makes a good digging tool. With an axe, a blunt, chisel-shaped point can be cut at one end. Once the pit is complete, it would be lined with flat stones that would later radiate heat back into the meat.

A fire was set in the pit and, after a couple of hours, was raked back with the digging sticks. It will have been wasteful not to reuse the embers, and so it made sense to build a new fire next to the earth oven on which other foods could be cooked while the joint was roasting nicely in the ground. The meat will have been simply laid onto the hot stones unprotected, but then covered with a simple latticework of twigs and branches. On top of this, large damp clumps of moss, which were available throughout the Mesolithic forest, were then piled up several layers deep. Finally, any soil left over from the excavation of the pit could have been added to the pile, further insulating the meat as it cooked. Within two or three hours the men would have uncovered their roasted venison and shared the feast with the rest of the family. The building of an earth oven was best done by many hands, and those hands all expected to be fed at the end of it all.

Burnt Mounds

British archaeologists have identified a common prehistoric feature that they term the 'burnt mound'. Burnt mounds are large oval or crescent-shaped piles of fire-cracked stone. These structures are typically found on the banks of fast-flowing streams as well as adjacent to some sort of clay or wood-lined water pit. Burnt mounds are typically found in highland areas, usually in the north and west of Britain. Most are found in Scotland, but this may simply reflect the intensive cultivation (and thus destruction of such mounds) carried out in the lowlands of Britain. Nearly all were deposited during the Bronze Age, although a small number have been dated to the Neolithic.

Archaeologists have identified the water pits as locations for the heating of water and determined that the fire-cracked stones were part of this process. Initially heated in the fire, the stones were then dropped one at a time into the

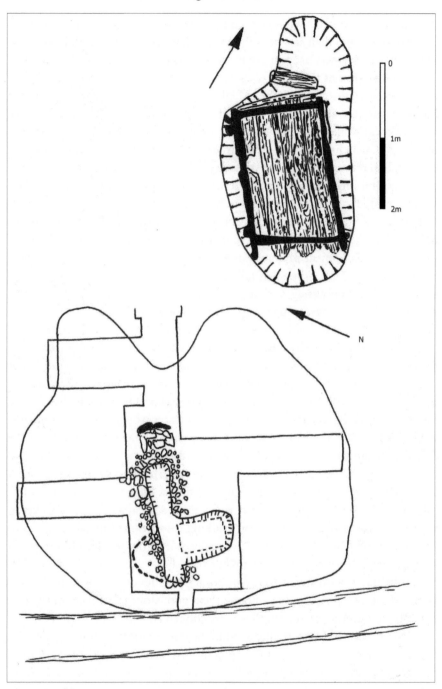

Burnt Mounds.
Top: Wooden trough for boiling water at Killeens, County Cork.
Bottom: Excavated *fulacht fiadh*, showing excavated mound, troughs, and stream, Ballyvourney, County Cork.
(*C. Burgess*)

lined pit until the water within began to boil. Theories around the purpose of burnt mounds and their use in boiling water have polarized around two main ideas: that water was used to create steam inside an American Indian-style 'sweat lodge' or that the water was used either in cooking or brewing. When the stones were thrown into the trough they passed their heat into the water, but were often shattered as a result of the great temperature change. Once the work was done, the cracked stones were scooped out and thrown onto a nearby pile, which inevitably grew larger over time. This is the burnt mound that is observed by archaeologists today. The presence of a mound suggests that the water pits were not designed for a single event, but were used to boil water repeatedly, on many different occasions.

The Greek scholar Athenaeus, quoting the earlier writer Poseidonios, tells us that the food of the Celts 'consists of a few loaves of bread and of large quantities of meat prepared in water or roasted over coals or on spits' (Athenaeus 4.151). Is Athenaeus talking about cooking meat in a water pit? If so, it would certainly suggest that the burnt mound deposits found in Britain and Ireland were cooking apparatus, rather than sweat lodges.

In Ireland, burnt mounds are known as *fulachta fiadh*. Famously, in 1954, Professor Michael O'Kelly constructed his own water pit in order to test the hypothesis that burnt mounds were the product of cooking. By adding fire heated stones to the water, Professor Kelly was able to bring the water slowly to the boil. His pebbles were heated in a fire that had been built close to the pit and they were transferred from log fire to water trough using a dampened wooden shovel. In this way, the water temperature was maintained and the 5-kg leg of mutton he was cooking was ready to eat after three hours and forty minutes. What had at first seemed like a perfectly sized pit for the task at hand was, by the end of the experiment, almost full of ash and stones. The ash had little effect on the meat that was wrapped up in a protective jacket of straw. The use of straw in water pit cooking is mentioned in *The History of Ireland*, dating from 1908. In it, the servants of Irish hunters build a couple of fires and begin heating stones, meanwhile they dig two pits close by. Next they 'bind [the meat] with sugans (grasses) in dry bundles and set it to boil in the larger of the two pits, and keep plying them with stones that were in the fire, making them seethe often until they were cooked'.

Grass or straw is tightly bound around the joint of meat with string. Pebbles that are either igneous or metamorphic are needed to heat the water, since rocks such as shale or sandstone will split and break under intense heat. After about an hour in the fire the stones can be transferred to the water pit and this is done one at a time, giving each stone ample time to transfer its heat to the water. It takes around quarter of an hour for a good-sized stone to do this with the aim of boiling water, at which point the grass-shrouded meat is lowered into the pit. Stones are continually added to maintain a simmer.

Two or three hours should be sufficient time for the cooking process, after which the joint is brought to the surface.

Artefacts called 'flesh hooks' by archaeologists have been recovered from some Bronze Age and Iron Age sites. A fine example, discovered by Irish turf cutters at Dunaverney in 1829, had an oak handle decorated with bronze birds. At its tip sat two bronze hooks. In Little Thetford, Cambridgeshire, a similar flesh hook was discovered and although its wooden handle had not survived, a socketed metal end sporting two hooks, which would have been used to lift a joint of meat out of the water, was recovered. A rounded bronze cap decorated the opposite end of the instrument. Undoubtedly, these hooks were used to pull cooked meats from both water pits and from metal cauldrons that hung over roundhouse hearths. They are indicative of wealth and status, an item that was flashy and not just utilitarian. They also suggest that water-pit cooking, as well as the boiling of meat in cauldrons, was a social event, a feast with guests to both feed and impress.

> But among the [Celts of Galatia], says Phylarchus in his sixth book, it is the custom to place on the tables a great number of loaves broken plentifully, and meat just taken out of the cauldrons...

> Athenaeus 4.34

It is interesting to note that the introduction of large bronze, and later iron, cauldrons for the boiling of meat, replaced the need for water pit cooking. Vessels like the bronze Battersea cauldron are found throughout Britain and on the continent. Dating from the Early Iron Age, the Battersea cauldron was found in the River Thames, it stands 40 cm high and has a diameter of 56 cm. The cauldron is generally representative of the types and sizes of feasting cauldrons used in both the Late Bronze Age and throughout the Iron Age. There was no need for heated stones here, the cauldron hung by a chain from the rafters of the chief's roundhouse and boasted to everyone seated around it of the wealth of its owner. Of course the community at large would not have been invited to these feasts, the intended audience of the chief was his own following of warriors (his

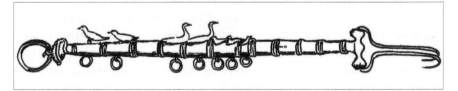

Bronze flesh hook from Dunaverney, County Antrim, used to pull joints of meat from cauldrons or water troughs. This was a mark of wealth, akin to the modern aristocrat's 'family silver'; it is intricately decorated with rows of birds.

war band) as well as important visitors. Iron Age cauldrons were symbols as well as cookpots; in Irish mythology the Dagda, one of the greatest of the Celtic gods, owned a huge magical cauldron. Warriors who had been killed in battle were lowered into the cauldron in order that they might be brought back to life.

The burnt mound structures that have such a wide distribution, in both area and time, will have served the communities that were responsible for their deposition. Just as with the traditional Hawaiian feast called the *luau*, complete with its earth oven-roasted pig, the Celtic water pit was probably the focus of community celebration. Funerals, marriages, victories, and other important events would be marked with a communal feast, and, as with the *luau*, everyone will have chipped in to get it ready.

On a much smaller domestic scale, stones can be used to heat up liquids in bowls and cooking pots. Heaps of heat-shattered pebbles are often found on Dartmoor, associated with the cooking hearths of Bronze Age roundhouses. It isn't large joints of meat that are being cooked here, but instead soups or other preparations, away from the fire. The pebbles that are being heated in the hearth are removed from the fire with wooden batons or tongs. Milk can be heated like this in order to make soft cheese (see Chapter 8), and both soups and pottages can be cooked quite easily. By far the most compelling reasons for the use of these 'pot-boilers' is the ability to cook foods in wooden bowls and also to be able to cook away from the fire. When meat is being spit roasted or grilled over the flames, and when havercakes and flat breads are baking on fireside stones, space at the hearth would be at a premium. Fire-heated pebbles carry the energy of the fire with them and must be dropped into the pot at regular intervals, rather than all at once. The goal is to keep the food at a gentle simmer. I have found that it is best to pour the cooked contents of the pot into a large wooden bowl ready for dishing out, as this allows the pebbles to be dried and then dumped back into the fire if needed.

Bread Stones

At the Iron Age village of Glastonbury an unusual doughnut-shaped piece of bread was discovered. It has been suggested that this bread was baked using a hot stone. The technique, when I tried it, proved extremely simple. Dough is rolled out into a rectangle about a centimetre thick and long enough to wrap around the fire stone. This stone is heated for a good thirty minutes in the hearth and then brought across with wooden tongs to be carefully placed into the centre of the dough. Quickly, so as to not lose any of the heat, the dough is then rolled around the stone to form a doughnut. The bread is left to bake for an hour or two until the heat dissipates completely. Obviously the dough touching the stone is burnt and inedible, but the rest of the loaf certainly claims the definition of bread.

12

FEASTING AND DRINKING

The drink of the wealthy is wine imported from Italy.... This is unmixed, but sometimes a little water is added. The lower classes drink a beer made from wheat...

Athenaeus 4.36

While the Greeks came together in the wine-drinking *symposion* and the Romans gorged themselves within their private *triclinia*, Celtic warriors and their chiefs lived for the feast. The literary theme of the drunken Celt was a common one in the ancient world, but there are enough observations of barbarian drinking and feasting by authors like Polybius, Dionysus, and Strabo to give us a good idea of what occurred at these events.

At the Feast

According to some of these ancient authors, although barbarian Celts were known to eat voraciously, they still maintained a certain etiquette while feasting.

They eat their meat in a cleanly manner enough, but like lions, taking up whole joints in both their hands and gnawing them; and if there is any which they cannot easily tear away, they cut it off with a small blade.

Athenaeus 4.36

Guests and hosts, alike, were seated not on chairs, but on the ground using wolf skins or other animal hides as cushions. Some lay hay on the floor and sat on that. The food and drink was served on little wooden tables raised slightly off of the ground. If the customs of the Celtic Galatians were representative, then loaves of bread, broken and ready to eat, were placed on the tables along with meat that had been hooked out of the cauldrons or roasted on spits over the hearth. Food was served on plates of silver, bronze, or wood, or in woven baskets—as the wealth of the household dictated. Youths, both male and female, served up the food—Celtic society was not generally slave-owning and it is likely that these children were the chief's own daughters and foster-sons (sons were usually sent away to be brought up by a male relative or a trusted ally).

During formal gatherings or feasts, as in most social occasions, there was a precedence and a public recognition of status. The diners sat in a circle, with the chief or heroic warrior most likely sat opposite the doorway, behind the hearth. His warrior brothers, his attendants, and his guests were seated around the circle in a manner suggestive of the Arthurian Round Table. This arrangement seems to fit with our observations of life within the roundhouse, but there was in fact no tangible connection—Celts in Gaul, Iberia, and elsewhere on the continent dwelt in rectangular houses, rather than round ones. To be sat close to the chief was an honour. Strangers could be invited to the feast, but in common with other heroic societies of the ancient world, no one could ask these strangers about their business or intentions until after the meal. This was guest-friendship.

When drinking began, a cupbearer would pour wine from a jar of earthenware, silver, or bronze. Guests and fellow warriors alike had to be impressed with the feast and so for the richest Iron Age tribes of southern England, wine was the only drink on the menu. It was a luxury, imported by Roman merchants from southern Gaul and traded up the Rhône valley to Celtic tribes further north. Some of this wine made it across the Channel to Britain, and some of that made its way into elaborate Iron Age burials. A barrow burial at Lexden, near Colchester, for example, contained more than eighteen wine amphorae along with a host of expensive luxury goods. The chieftain buried at Welwyn, Hertfordshire, was accompanied on his journey to the Celtic otherworld by five amphorae of wine and all of the drinking cups, serving jugs, bowls, and plates he would need in order to host a grand feast. Each amphora of imported wine was paid for with a single human slave, probably captured from a rival tribe for that very purpose.

Wine was usually drunk unmixed or 'neat' as is the fashion today, but occasionally it was mixed with water, a practice that the Greeks and Romans found much more acceptable. It seems that drinks at a Celtic feast were served into a drinking bowl and passed around the circle, clockwise, with each diner taking only a mouthful, although they were known to take frequent draughts. Our own Iron Age feasts around the hearth often involved two bowls of mead being passed around the circle in opposite directions. In a wonderful touch of detail, Diodorus describes how the large moustaches of the Gallic aristocrats acted as strainers, through which the wine or beer was passed.

The wine bowl (or bowls) must have been passed around fairly frequently, because it is clear that the Celts were prone to squabbling and arguing at their feasts. Fights were also known to break out:

> And it is their custom, even during the course of the meal, to seize upon any trivial matter as an occasion for keen disputation and then to challenge one another to single combat, without any regard for their lives...

Diodorus 28

Nothing sparked the competitiveness and jealousy of a British or Gallic warrior more than missing out on the honour of the 'champion's portion'. The bravest warrior was traditionally awarded the choicest portion of meat and was slighted if he did not receive it. This was not some trivial fit of pique, but an act of face-saving; chiefs and warriors alike earned their position at a king's side through reputation and skill in war. A slight to their reputation could see their status fall, their followers melt away, and another, more fêted champion, rise to fill his position. And so it was that a piece of meat could cause the death of a man:

> There was a custom that a hind quarter of pork was put on the table and the bravest man took it; and if anyone else laid claim to it, then the two rose up to fight till one of them was slain.

Athenaeus 4.40

Stories of Irish heroes from this period refer to these honour fights for the champion's portion. Indeed, the tale of *Bricriu's Feast* tells of a plot by the eponymous nobleman, to set rival Ulster champions and their households against one another. He does this by telling each of his guests (Cúchulainn, Conall, and Lóegaire) as they enter his feasting hall, that they will be awarded the champion's portion. Of course all are furious when they discover that their rivals wish to take the portion of meat for themselves. All three champions then compete for the honour in a series of trials.

Some of the fighting was simply play, mock combat, and practice thrusts that might have developed during a heated discussion about a particular fight or sword technique. Even these displays might end in wounding, or even death—perhaps this was the drink at work. Polybius tells us that fighting at the dining table was made all the easier because the warriors usually ate and drank far too much.

Celtic Beer

Within the records of a Roman fort called Vindolanda, which sits along the line of Hadrian's Wall, a writing tablet recorded evidence of British beer-drinking around AD 100. Tablet 190 lists all manner of supplies, including Massic wine, sour wine, barley, pork fat, fish sauce, and *cervesae* or Celtic beer. The stuff was being purchased in batches of either 18 or 27 litres at a time, and it is clear that the soldiers (who were initially recruited in northern Europe along the Rhine) were keen beer drinkers. They would certainly have acquired a taste for beer in their homeland and this is reinforced by the urgent requests of a Roman officer in Tablet 628. Masculus, a cavalry decurion, asks his unit commander, Flavius Cerialis:

> Please, my lord, give instructions on what you want us to do tomorrow. Are we all to return with the standard, or just half of us? ... [missing lines] ... most fortunate and be well-disposed towards me. My fellow soldiers have no beer. Please order some to be sent.

Barbarian tastes for Celtic beer may have been satisfied by the local brews that were being produced by Britons who lived in the shadow of the Roman occupation forts. Despite the conquest of Rome and the defeat of the British tribes in AD 43, the inhabitants of Britain continued to live an essentially Late Iron Age existence. Away from the new Roman towns, where wine-drinking, fig-eating, and toga-wearing was catching on quickly, local farming communities continued to bake flat bread and brew barley beer within their roundhouses. This beer may have been transported to the thirsty Roman troops who were garrisoning the forts, or alternatively soldiers might actually have been brewing their own Celtic beer. There are references in the Vindolanda tablets to the profession of brewer (*cervesarii*) as well as to a *bracarius*—braces is thought to have been the Roman term for spelt wheat, a cereal known to have been used in the production of Celtic beer.

Athenaeus refers to the Gauls drinking wheat beer, sometimes with the added ingredient of honey, but it is clear from other writers like Diodorus, that beer was also made of barley. The Roman emperor Julian, ruling in the fourth century AD, looked down disdainfully on the beer that was drunk by his barbarian legionaries. In his poem to beer, Julian wrote that 'it was in their lack of grapes that the Celts brewed thee from corn-ears. So should we call thee Demetrius [after the grain god], not Dionysus [the grape god]'. Although he loved his Celtic legions, Emperor Julian did not like their beer and he describes the stuff as smelling like billy-goat.

Hard evidence of beer drinking comes from the Celtic site of Hochdorf, in south-western Germany. The chieftains of this community threw elaborate feasts and created a dedicated brewery designed to quench the thirst of their numerous guests. Six specially excavated ditches were dedicated to the brewing process and were found to contain thousands of charred and malted barley grains. This was a malt-making enterprise, a key part of beer brewing. Archaeologist Hans-Peter Sitka of the University of Hohenheim, Stuttgart, analysed the ancient techniques and then reconstructed the malting process.

The Hochdorf ditches were first used to soak the barley grains in order to encourage them to sprout. Next the grains were dried when fires were lit at the ends of each ditch, this process would have passed on to the grains a dark colour and a smoky taste. When the barley malt was slow dried, lactic acid bacteria would have gotten to work, adding a sourness to the brew. Hops were not used to flavour these ancient beers, instead plants such as mugwort, elderberry, heather, wild carrot, or henbane were put to use, ingredients that we know were favoured by Medieval brewers centuries later.

Sitka suggested that honey or fruit may have been added to the 'wort' (or liquefied malt), which will have brought with it wild yeasts to trigger the fermentation process. The wort had to be heated slowly, and the best way Celtic brewers could achieve this was through the application of fire-heated stones. It is likely that the burnt mound structures found across Britain were actually used for brewing beer, as well as for cooking joints of meat. In 2009, David Chapman, who had excavated a burnt mound on the Lleyn peninsula in Wales, decided to brew beer using the burnt mound as a guide. In replicating the process, he intended to compare the debris that resulted with the remains that he had excavated the previous year.

Chapman began by setting a large oak trough, one quarter of the size of the original, into a pit that had been sealed with clay. The water used to fill it had to be sterilised and to do that a bonfire was lit over a large pile of stones. Once these stones began to change colour (a sign that they had reached the required temperature) they were raked from the ashes and dropped into the trough. Next the stones were returned to the fire, ready for the next step in the process. Brewer's malted barley was drenched in some of the boiling water in order to release the starches within and then, once it had cooled sufficiently (60°C was considered sufficient) it was added to the water of the trough. This wort had to be held at 60°C for an hour and a half, and this was achieved by dropping in a heated pebble every ten minutes.

Chapman's team added elderberries to the mix, not just to flavour the beer, but to kick-start the fermentation. The skin of elderberry is one of the best sources of wild yeast in Europe. As a backup, a measure of brewer's yeast was also added. Other ingredients, including honey, rosehip, and blackberry, helped to flavour the beer.

At last the wort was strained through a fine cloth into wooden buckets, which were then set to cool in a nearby stream. After this, the contents were covered and the brew left to ferment for five days. In the true spirit of prehistoric reconstruction, Chapman did not throw out the mash that was left behind following the straining, instead he used it to bake bread on hot stones next to the fire. The beer produced at the end if this time consuming process amounted to seventy-seven pints of very drinkable light ale. What did the beer taste like? Experimental brewers like David Chapman are able to produce an ale without hops that has an unusual flavour, at least to the modern drinker, and a beer that is much cloudier than its modern equivalent, laden as it is with yeasty sediment.

Around the world today, beer is still produced by hand in small communities for purely local consumption. In the Tanzanian town of Manyara, just south of the Kenyan border, I was shown around a local drinking house. While most pubs and bars in the town served Western soft drinks or commercially produced bottled beers, this place brewed its own banana beer on site, using bananas from the plantation that I had just come from. A dusty courtyard contained the owner's house as well as a small shack at the back and a circular shelter with a banana-leaf roof and assorted chairs. This 'round house' served as the bar's main room.

My eye was attracted to the huge cauldron at the rear of the yard, within which a wort of banana beer was being slowly heated over a log fire. The brewer, a local Manyaran lady, stirred the wort continuously in the hot sun. The interior of the shack at the rear was small and dark, but it held a number of reused feed sacks, which were hanging from the roof. Each one contained a banana beer mash that was either being strained into a large aluminium pot, or had been strained and was now drying. It wasn't just the roundhouse-like lounge-bar of the place that had me thinking about brewers in prehistoric Britain, it was the small scale nature of the operation. Many of her customers were workers from the banana co-operative next door and it was with bananas from that same plantation that she used to brew her beer.

Although I doubt that any Celtic village ever boasted a street cafe like that in Manyara, they will certainly have engaged in local beer brewing— the remains of burnt mound structures bear witness to this. Here is a small scale, family run brewery, operating with a wood fire and shoe-string resources, to bring beer to dozens of local people. In Manyara, the drinking was reward for a tough day in the sun or part of a weekend reverie, but in Celtic Britain, the brewing may have been simply another aspect of the community's agricultural workload, along with hay harvests and lambing.

Beer was needed throughout the year as a drink for the family, it was both nutritious and free from the bacteria, which could infect fresh water; however, beer would also play an important part in the community's feasts and festivals.

Beer Flavourings

Although the term 'beer' is being used here, that drink is technically one made with the addition of hops. Before the introduction of beer-brewing and hops cultivation at the end of the fifteenth century, the native malted alcoholic drink of England was known as an 'ale'. Hops provided a new and novel bitter taste; its popularity was not based on flavour alone, but also on its qualities of preservation that help to extend the life of beer. Prior to the sixteenth century, a variety of indigenous herbs and plants were used to flavour ale, and this combination of herbs was called 'gruit'. In prehistory, the components of a gruit will have varied from region to region and from tradition to tradition. Medieval brewers could choose from a host of native ingredients to add to their ale including juniper berry, sweet gale, ground ivy, mugwort, seaweed, meadowsweet, elderberry, yarrow, horehound, heather, and even seaweed.

Mead

Mead predates both wine and beer and as such it represents the oldest known form of alcoholic drink in Europe. Since neither grapes nor cereal crop is required in its production it is likely that hunter-gatherer societies across Europe and Africa enjoyed this delicious drink. Mead is based around the fermentation of honey and seems to have been popular among the prehistoric societies of northern Europe, where wine production was always hampered by the climate. Elegant Beaker pottery that spread across Early Bronze Age Europe is thought to have brought with it both a taste for mead and a culture of mead drinking. Prior to the mechanized extraction of honey from the honeycomb in the nineteenth century, the combs were crushed and flushed with warm water in order to gain access to the honey within. The water that remained became the base for the production of mead. Classical writers Aristotle and Pliny both mention the drinking of mead and, although Romans generally favoured wine at their banquets, Columella published his own recipe for mead that used grape must as a base.

Mead drinking is associated with the Saxons and Vikings, who enjoyed the drink in their mead halls. Celtic chiefs and heroes were also fond of mead, as the British poet Taliesin attests in his poem called 'Song to Mead'. Taliesin was a British poet and bard who lived around AD 600, two centuries after the end of Roman rule. Lines in the poem capture the love that the ancient Britons had for this drink:

> *May Maelgwn of Môn be drunk with mead and us likewise*
> *From frothing horns of finest purest mead*
> *Which bees collect but ne'er enjoy.*
> *Mead refined, glistening is everywhere praised.*

'Song to Mead', *Book of Taliesin*, 19

The drinking, feasting, and boasting of Celtic warriors who enjoyed the pleasures of their chief's hospitality is conjured vividly in the mead hall of Din Eidyn (modern day Edinburgh) as it appears in Y Gododdin. This poem, written by Aneirin, a contemporary of Taliesin, refers to mead many times. The warriors loyal to Mynyddog Mwynfawr, chief of the Gododdin tribe were treated to a whole year of feasting and mead-drinking before they launched a heroic attack on the rival kingdom of the Angles further south:

> *Men went to Catraeth at morn*
> *Their high spirits lessened their life-span*
> *They drank mead, gold and sweet, ensnaring;*
> *For a year the minstrels were merry.*
> *Red their swords, let the blades remain*
> *Uncleansed, white shields and four-sided spearheads,*
> *Before Mynyddog Mwynfawr's men.*

Aneirin, 'Y Gododdin' 13

The Roman Invasion

Boiled Chicken in its own Broth:

Crush pepper, cumin, a little thyme, fennel seed, mint, rue and asafoetida root, moisten with vinegar and add dates. Work well and make it savoury with honey, vinegar, broth and oil to taste: the boiled chicken properly cleaned and dried is covered with this sauce.

Apicius 6

With the arrival of the Roman army in AD 43, the everyday diet of the British people was transformed forever. Officers and administrators brought with them their beliefs and fashions as well as their tastes in food. No doubt they dined well, just as they had been accustomed to, with their cooks taking recipes and culinary tips from the book of Apicius, a Roman gourmet. Along with these administrators came Roman spices and herbs, such as cumin, pepper, and thyme and an entire kitchen-full of new vegetables and fruits that would all eventually take root in British soil. Romanization meant the adoption of Roman customs and ways of living in the new Roman towns that had been established following the conquest and pacification of Britain. Roman foods were in demand, not just in the street cafes and taverns of Londinium and Verulamium, but in peoples' homes.

New Tastes, New Crops

Of course the biggest impact on British palates would be the exotic spices and fragrant herbs that now reached the British Isles from all parts of the Roman Empire and beyond. Pepper, ginger, saffron, and cumin came from the East, whilst thyme, dill, fennel, rosemary, and sage were transported from the Mediterranean. With these flavourings, dishes began to take on a whole new dimension and with the addition of both honey and wine vinegar (often together in the same recipe), they could boast a uniquely Roman sweet-and-sour quality.

Throughout the Roman occupation of Britain, however, these spices and herbs always remained an exotic import. Although they did have their role to play in the new Roman diet, it must have been the vegetables that were introduced to British farmers that had the greatest impact in the countryside. Here were new foods and new crops, and they could be grown on British farms. We have the Romans to thank for cabbage, parsnip, broad bean, beetroot, radish, asparagus, and an improved (edible) variety of carrot. Excavations at Silchester have uncovered evidence for the consumption and probable cultivation of all these vegetables. Celery seeds were also found there as well as at sites further north. Some foods, like lettuce and cucumber, which today we consider to be a salad food, were introduced by the Romans as something to be cooked before eating. The cabbage was a particular favourite of Roman diners and there were more than a dozen varieties. Cato asserted that it is 'the cabbage which surpasses all other vegetables; it promotes digestion marvellously and is an excellent laxative' (Cato, On Agriculture, 156).

Fruits were also imported to Britain and they have remained here ever since. Plums and cherries left behind stones, which have been found at places like Doncaster, London, and Chew Park in Gloucestershire. Other fruits included pears, mulberries, gooseberries, and new varieties of apple that were far more edible than the sour native crab apple. Techniques of grafting were well-known to Roman farmers and the new species would have been grafted onto indigenous crab apple trees.

There were some fruits that could not make a permanent transition across the Channel. Figs were eaten with relish in Roman Britain, as the many fig seeds at Silchester, York, and Verulamium attest. Dates have also been found in Colchester (carbonised in the destructive fires set by Boudiccan rebels). Both fruits were dried and imported in large amphorae. While almonds and walnuts only ever made their way to Britain in the holds of cargo ships, the chestnut was cultivated successfully in Roman Britain and has remained a part of the British diet ever since. Chestnuts were eaten raw, but could also be fed to animals or ground into flour and used in baking.

Olive oil certainly influenced the diet of Romanised Britons. It replaced lard for cooking and tallow as a method of fuelling lamps. Of course, olive oil also features as an ingredient in many of the Apician dishes. Like dried figs and dates, the oil was shipped across to Britain in bulk, sealed in large clay amphorae that were stacked on the decks of Gallic sailing ships. These hard-wearing pottery vessels also introduced another Roman delicacy to the British palate—*garum*, or fish sauce. This popular condiment actually came in a number of grades: *liquamen, garum, muria,* and *allec,* all of which were the product of fermenting the guts and off-cuts of fish in the Mediterranean sun. *Garum* resembled the *nuoc mam* or *nam pla* that features so centrally within Vietnamese and Thai cookery. Evidence from amphorae shards found at

London, Colchester, York, and Gloucester indicate that *garum* was certainly part of the Romano-British diet.

Although some wines might have been made by prehistoric Britons using the native fruits available to them, the ancient Greek and Roman authors make it clear that the drink of the Celts was beer. That changed with the coming of Rome, and those that could afford it now drank wines imported from southern Gaul, Hispania, and other parts of the Mediterranean. One amphora tag, found at Richborough fort in southern England, had come from vineyards growing on the slopes of Mount Vesuvius, on the Bay of Naples. Wine also arrived from other parts of Italy, from Rhodes, and (later) from vineyards in North Africa. The numerous shards of excavated wine amphorae suggest that much of this wine trade passed through the port of Londinium. In addition to the amphorae, wooden barrels were used to carry wine from supplier to buyer across parts of northern Europe. Several barrel staves were found at the Roman fort of Vindolanda, some of which carried inscriptions that indicated a source for the wine in Gaul or the German Rhineland. Archaeologists have searched for evidence of viticulture in Roman Britain, but most of the finds have been somewhat ambiguous. The best evidence so far has been that of grapevine pollen found in soil at Wollaton, Nottinghamshire, and at Irchester, Somerset.

Romanisation among the Britons was neither inevitable nor complete. Those tribes forced to relocate from hill forts into towns readily adopted Roman customs, fashions, and habits. Those Britons living in the countryside, tending crops and flocks away from Roman villa estates and the bustle of city life, remained relatively untouched. Taxes had to be paid, of course, and, like any community in a developing nation today, there were always useful new products that could be purchased from the townsfolk. Roman-style pottery replaced Iron Age ware, for example, and imported vegetable crops like cabbage and lettuce began to appear in the pollen record.

Roman Farming

Just as cattle and sheep crossed the Channel at the beginning of the Neolithic, they began to do so again under Roman rule. This time improved varieties were introduced. White-fleeced sheep were set to graze on the uplands of Britain, replacing the brown-fleeced Soay and Mouflon-type breeds of the prehistoric period. The white fleeces were popular amongst Romano-British farmers since they made dying much easier and put more meat on the table.

In the area of improved technologies, the large two-handed scythe allowed for a much greater quantity of hay to be harvested efficiently. There were metallurgical improvements in axes, sickles, spades, saws, and mattocks, making work a little easier—and therefore faster. The new breeds of sheep required shears with which to shear them, and Roman spring-loaded iron shears were introduced to fulfil this role.

Perhaps the greatest innovation was the use of a heavier type of plough with a coulter for cutting into the soil and with a share and mould board, which enabled the furrow to be turned. This will have allowed Romano-British farmers to open up new areas of farmland. Although most farmers had previously been engaged in purely subsistence agriculture, the existence of a market, with thousands of hungry city dwellers and soldiers in garrison, would have spurred on new land clearance. Following Julius Caesar's raids on the south east of Britain and the imposition of a corn requisition on the local tribes, wheat soon became one of Britain's main exports as the natives began to open up previously uncultivated farmland. The *annona militaris*, or corn tax, forced some of this increased wheat production. Subsistence farmers now had to farm more land and produce more wheat just in order to fulfil their obligations to the *annona militaris*. Those with extra capacity were able to extend their production still further, leading to a profitable asset.

That farmers could improve their lot is proven in the archaeology of Roman villas, many of which began life as small rectangular Roman-style cottages. Over the course of several generations these expanded to become impressive villa complexes in their own right. Some of these great farming estates were not the country seat of a wealthy Roman nobleman, or of some Romanized chief, but the hard-won fruits of a family farm that had prospered through the decades. Villas were an unfamiliar sight to prehistoric eyes, but they would eventually spread across the length and breadth of southern and central Britain. Typically associated mainly with an impressive tiled building, often with one or more wings, a bathhouse, underfloor heating, and an impressive mosaic floor, villas were actually farming estates, akin to the manor houses of the eighteenth century.

NATIVE PLANT SPECIES

It was only after I began trying to recreate ancient cookery techniques that I realised how small the choice of ingredients was for the prehistoric cook. Of course there were no tomatoes or potatoes, nothing from the Americas, but a great many British staples had also yet to be introduced. Some of these familiar vegetables, like the asparagus and cabbage, were introduced by the Romans, while others (broccoli, spinach, and cauliflower, for example) appeared on British plates centuries later.

The two lists of edible plants in this appendix, Native Food Plants and Later Arrivals, provide a comparison (and a shocking one) that illustrates how little of the food modern Britons consume today is actually native to these islands. Both lists use data from the Archaeobotanical Computer Database (ABCD) as interpreted by archaeologists Philippa Tomlinson and Allan Hall. Some of the evidence for seed remains is ambiguous, and I have had to tread carefully in trying to provide a balanced summary of what was being thrown into roundhouse cookpots. A single grape seed has been found dated to the Neolithic, for example, but I have not put grape on to the Native Food Plant List. Conversely no seeds of hemp have been found prior to the Roman invasion, but hemp pollen 'has' been discovered on prehistoric sites, and so hemp has been included. A number of other examples of archaeobotanical data have had to be carefully weighed. Take beetroot, for example; although two finds from Roman York were identified, the dig reports associate them with dumping grounds. The final analysis determined that cattle or sheep had perhaps grazed on the native wild plant sea beet (a wild variety of beetroot), which grows in coastal salt marsh.

Absent from the lists are those plants that a modern Briton would today consider a weed. In the past, and not just the prehistoric past, many of these weeds were harvested, processed, and eaten. It is likely that some wild plants, particularly fat-hen, were actively cultivated and formed an important part of the prehistoric diet. When one looks at the tiny number of native vegetables available to the roundhouse cook, it becomes obvious that alternatives must have been exploited. Ray Mears and Gordon Hillman, in their book *Wild*

Food, provide an extensive and in-depth analysis of edible British plants, from root to seed and leaf to stalk. It is staggering how much of the plant life growing wild in woods and hedgerows today is edible, and Mesolithic communities will have exploited it to the full. With the spread of cereal and livestock farming, dependence switched to cultivated crops, but many wild plants will have continued to have been harvested and used to provide the nutrients that the cereal diet lacked. Fat-hen, pig nut, nettle, shepherd's purse, red deadnettle, and many other so-called 'weeds' are all perfectly edible and make a tasty addition to a stew or soup. The 'growing grounds' or kitchen gardens that have been proposed by archaeologist Francis Pryor may even have been used to cultivate some of these wild plants.

Native Food Plants

Berries
Hawthorn
Wild Strawberry
Rosehip
Dewberry
Bramble
Raspberry
Blackcurrant
Elderberry
Rowan

Other Fruits
Crab Apple
Sloe

Vegetables
Turnip
Wild Carrot

Pulses
Pea
Celtic or Field Bean

Herbs & Flavourings
Savory

Oil-bearing Plants
Flax Seed
Hemp
Opium Poppy

Cereals
Oats
Barley
Bread Wheat
Emmer
Spelt

Nuts
Hazelnuts

Later Arrivals

Berries
Gooseberry
Bilberry

Other Fruits
Quince
Fig
Medlar
Olive
Mulberry
Date
Cherry
Plum
Peach
Pear
Grape
Banana
Lemon
Orange
Pineapple
Rhubarb
Watermelon

Vegetables

Beetroot
Onion
Parsnips
Celery
Leek
Cabbage
Spinach
Asparagus
Chard
Marrow
Cucumber
Domesticated Carrot
Broccoli
Brussel Sprout
Potato
Tomato
Cauliflower
Lettuce
Spinach
Runner Bean
Radish

Pulses

Lentil
Broad Bean

Herbs & Flavourings

Garlic
Pepper
Chilli
Celery Seed
Borage
Chervil
Coriander
Fennel
Hop
Hyssop
Garden Cress
Marjoram

Parsley
Alexander
Cocoa Bean

Oil-bearing Plants
Gold-of-Pleasure
Olive

Cereals
Buckwheat
Millet
Durum Wheat

Nuts
Walnut
Almond
Pine Nut
Chestnut
Peanut

Experimental Data

It would be fascinating to step back in time to walk the field boundaries and examine the amount of food produced in a typical Bronze Age farm. Exactly how many people could a farm feed? What was the annual crop yield? What size herd of cattle could this hypothetical farm support? Professor Roger Mercer, who has excavated sites such as Hambledon Hill and Carn Brea, has used evidence from a nineteenth century agricultural treatise as well as the findings of Butser Ancient Farm and evidence from prehistoric sites to suggest possible levels of agricultural production in British prehistory. His findings were speculative, but help to provide a sense of scale and population, putting a little 'meat' on to the archaeological 'bones'.

The Butser data was found to resemble figures of agricultural production from eighteenth century England, which provided some confidence when turning to the Butser farm for useful (and quantifiable) information. Land area is measured in hectares; visualise a hectare by imagining a square field with edges 100 m in length. A single edge of the field can be walked in about a minute, whilst the perimeter of the entire field can be walked in four to five minutes.

Experiments at Butser illustrated that the production of winter sown emmer varied, but averaged about 1.85 tons per annum, per hectare. This is an average, the Butser results actually varied from 3.7–0.4 tons per hectare, and the wheat grew on a north-facing slope without the benefit of manure. Assuming a wastage level due to rotting, disease, etc. (which approximates to 20 per cent) we are left with an annual wheat harvest of around 1.48 tons per hectare.

Analysis of Victorian agricultural practice, as well as the results of Butser's own findings, suggest that the proportion of grain that must be set aside as seed corn for the next round of sowing was 3 per cent. Mercer erred on the side of caution, however, and assumed that 5 per cent of the harvest was put into storage as seed corn, again compensating for some spoilage and spillage of the seed.

The 1885 *Notebook of Agricultural Facts and Figures* states that one ton of threshed grain occupies 1.15 m³. This is roughly comparable to the capacity of most prehistoric beehive and bell-shaped storage pits (which have a standard volume of 1.2 m³, equating to 1.12 tons of grain). Each of these grain pits could therefore hold the produce of three-quarters of a hectare. According to Roger Mercer, it is likely that the wooden granaries, raised on posts, held a similar amount.

One kilogram of emmer wheat can be ground down to 900 g of flour, which provides around 3,100 calories. The UK National Health Service states that a man requires around 2,500 calories per day and a woman requires around 2,000 calories. In addition, an active ten year old requires about the same calories each day as an adult woman. A family of husband, wife, and two ten-year-old children would therefore require 8,500 calories per day. If surviving on bread alone, this family would need almost 3 kg of wheat to be ground at the quernstone each day. Of course the family's calorific intake was supplemented by a host of other food sources, from beer to hazelnuts, nettle soup to roast duck. In the main, however, bread and the cereal crop has formed the staple food for the poor agricultural majority of most preindustrial societies.

Adding weight to these numbers is the fact that Roman soldiers were allocated one third of a ton of wheat over the course of a year, which equates to the accepted Standard Nutritional Unit of 1 million calories per annum. This provides a useful value for calculating the amount of cultivated land required to support one adult. On these figures, one year's worth of wheat for one person relied on the cultivation of 0.22 hectares of cropland. Should our family of four live on bread alone, it would require 1 ton of cereal grain to be reaped each year for its survival. A harvest of this size required about two-thirds of a hectare of land to be put under cultivation.

How would our family store their harvest? Most excavated grain pits could store a ton of threshed grain, although it is likely that the Britons stored their harvest as un-threshed ears of corn. The raised timber granaries, which have left neat pairs of post-holes in many roundhouse yards, are thought to have held a similar amount to the grain pits. For a family of four, then, a couple of raised granaries or grain pits might well have served to store the annual harvest.

BIBLIOGRAPHY

Alcock, J., *Food in Roman Britain*, (The History Press, 2001)

Bottero, J., *The Oldest Cuisine in the World: Cooking in Mesopotamia*, (University of Chicago Press, 2011)

Bowman, S., and Needham, S., 'The Dunaverney and Little Thetford Flesh Hooks: History, Technology and their Position Within the Later Bronze Age Atlantic Zone Feasting Complex', *The Antiquaries Journal*, 87, pp. 53-108 (2007)

Bradley, R. J., *The Prehistory of Britain and Ireland*, (Cambridge University Press, 2007); *The Significance of Monuments*, (Routledge, 1998)

Burgess, C., *The Age of Stonehenge*, (J.M. Dent & Sons, 1980)

Clark, C., and Haswell, M., *The Economics of Subsistence Agriculture*, (Macmillan, 1964)

Coles, B. J., and Coles, J. M., *Sweet Track to Glastonbury: The Somerset Levels in Prehistory*, (Thames & Hudson, 1986)

Cunliffe, B., *Iron Age Britain*, (B.T. Batsford/English Heritage, 1995); *Iron Age Communities in Britain*, 4th edn, (Oxford University Press, 2004)

Edmunds, M., *Ancestral Geographies of the Neolithic*, (Routledge, 1999)

Ellis, C., Powell, A. B., and Hawkes, J., *An Iron Age Settlement Outside Battlesbury Hillfort, Warminster, and Sites along the Southern Range Road*, (Wessex Archaeology, 2008)

Fitzpatrick, A. P., 'The Amesbury Archer: A Well Furnished Early Bronze Age Burial in Southern England', *Antiquity*, Vol. 76, No. 293, pp. 629-30, (2002)

Fowler, P. J., *The Farming of Prehistoric Britain*, (Cambridge University Press, 1983)

Glob, P. V., *The Bog People*, (HarperCollins, 1971)

Grainger, S., *Cooking Apicius*, (Prospect Books, 2006)

Hunter, F., 'Excavations of an Early Bronze Age cemetery and other sites at West Water Reservoir, West Linton, Scottish Borders', *Proceedings of the Society of Antiquaries of Scotland*, 113, pp. 115-182, (2000)

King, J., *The Celtic Druid's Year*, (Cassell, 1995)

Mahon, B., *Land of Milk and Honey: The Story of Traditional Irish Food and*

Drink, (Mercier Press, 1998)

Malone, C., *Neolithic Britain and Ireland*, (Tempus, 2001)

Marcoux, P., *Cooking with Fire*, (Storey, 2014)

Mears, R., and Hillman, G., *Wild Food*, (Hodder & Stoughton, 2007)

Mercer, R. (ed.), *Farming Practice in British Prehistory*, (Edinburgh University Press, 1981)

Milner, N., Taylor, B., Conneller, C., and Schadla-Hall, T., *Star Carr: Life in Britain After the Ice Age*, (Council for British Archaeology, 2013)

Olmsted, G., *The Gaulish Calendar: A Reconstruction from the Bronze Fragments from Coligny, with an Analysis of its Function as a Highly Accurate Lunar-solar Predictor, as well as an Explanation of its Terminology and Development*, (R. Habelt, 1992)

Payne, F. G., 'The British Plough: Some Stages of Development', *Agricultural History Review*, 5, pp. 74-84. (1957)

Pearson, M. P., *Bronze Age Britain*, (B.T.Batsford/English Heritage, 1993)

Pryor, F., *Farmers in Prehistoric Britain*, (Tempus, 1999); *Home*, (Allen Lane, 2014)

Renfrew, J., *Food and Cooking in Prehistoric Britain*, (English Heritage, 1985)

Reynolds, D. M., 'Aspects of Later Timber Construction in south-east Scotland', in D. W. Harding (ed.), *Later Prehistoric Settlement in South-east Scotland*, University of Edinburgh Occasional Paper 8, pp. 44-56, (1982)

Reynolds, P. J., *Ancient Farming*, (Shire, 1987)

Sahlins, M., *Stone Age Economics*, (Tavistock Publications, 1974)

Stone, J. F. S., *Wessex*, (Thames & Hudson, 1958)

Tomlinson, P., and Hall, A., 'A review of the archaeological evidence for food plants from the British Isles: an example of the use of the Archaeobotanical Computer Database (ABCD)' in Issue 1, *Internet Archaeology*, (1996)

White, F., *Good Things in England: A Practical Cookery Book for Everyday Use*, (Jonathan Cape, 1932)

Wood, J., *Prehistoric Cooking*, (Tempus, 2001)

INDEX